250

FACES OF LATIN AMERICAN PROTESTANTISM

Faces of Latin American Protestantism

1993 Carnahan Lectures

José Míguez Bonino

Translated by
Eugene L. Stockwell

WILLIAM B. EERDMANS PUBLISHING COMPANY
GRAND RAPIDS, MICHIGAN / CAMBRIDGE, U.K.

Originally published as *Rostros del Protestantismo Latinoamericano*
by Wm. B. Eerdmans Publishing Co., 1995

This translation © 1997 Wm. B. Eerdmans Publishing Co.
255 Jefferson Ave. S.E., Grand Rapids, Michigan 49503 /
P.O. Box 163, Cambridge CB3 9PU U.K.

Printed in the United States of America

02 01 00 99 98 97   7 6 5 4 3 2 1

Library of Congress Cataloging-in-Publication Data

Míguez Bonino, José.
    Faces of Latin American protestantism: 1993 Carnahan lectures /
José Míguez Bonino.
        p.   cm.
    Includes bibliographical references.
    ISBN 0-8028-4225-9 (pbk.: alk. paper)
    1. Protestantism — 20th century. 2. Latin America — Church history —
20th century. 3. Liberation theology. 4. Evangelicalism — Latin America.
5. Pentecostalism — Latin America. 6. Fundamentalism — Latin America.
I. Title.
BX4805.2.M54 1997
280′.4′08 — dc20   96-43369
                                                              CIP

Contents

Preface

THE UNEXPECTED INVITATION to deliver the 1993 Carnahan Lectures was the temptation that gave birth to this book. No particular subject was indicated or suggested, but there was the supposition that it might have to do with "some theological topic of your interest, on which you are working," as is often stated in such invitation letters. The theme I finally settled on — given the pressure to announce the lectures — is one in which I am interested. To be more exact, it is almost an obsession. But it is not a subject on which I have worked profoundly and systematically. Furthermore, it cuts across areas of church history, the history of theology, systematic theology, and social interpretation. This lack of precision frees me from adhering to a strict methodology but seriously exposes me to improvisation and superficiality. Even so, passion won out over wisdom, and thus these lectures and this book came to be.

Only when I began to bog down in new paths, in the search for thematic directions, and in the need to plunge into unfamiliar topics and histories did I ask myself what malicious spirit had tempted me. I am not given to introspection — perhaps for fear of what I might discover — but I came to the conclusion that two issues are probably responsible for the choice of this topic. Both are shamefully subjective. The first is the necessity, which in truth I had never felt explicitly, to clarify for myself my own confessional and doctrinal identity. Here I came upon a surprise. I have been variously tagged a conservative, a revolutionary, a Barthian, a liberal, a catholic, a "moderate," and a liberationist. Probably there is truth in all of these. It is not for me to decide. However, when I do attempt to define myself in my innermost being, what "comes from within" is that I am *evangélico*. It seems that it is in this soil that my religious life and ecclesiastical activity have been rooted throughout more than seventy years. From this origin have sprung the joys and the conflicts, the satisfactions and the frustrations which over time have been knit together. There my deepest friendships, and also the most painful separations, were engendered; there lie the memories of dead ones I loved and the hope of generations I have seen born and grow. Whether in truth I am an *evangélico* is not for me to say. Nor am I concerned that others affirm or deny it. What I truly am belongs to the grace of God. At least an *evangélico* is what I have always wanted to be.

However, things are not so simple, and here my second issue arises. What does it mean to be *evangélico*? Moreover, what does it mean to be a contemporary Latin American *evangélico*? Nothing here is very clear. On the one hand, we would have to search out our histories: Where do we come from? Some of these histories — for example, those of classical Protestantism or those of the Catholicism against whose background we have defined our profiles — I have studied with some care. Others — particularly the spiritual, theological, and social trajectories of the Anglo-Saxon Protestant world — I know only in broad lines. (The preparation of these lectures forced me to learn more about them.) There are still others — those not yet written about our Latin American Protestant churches and religious movements — that are only beginning to appear in the current research of young historians. And what of the theology of Latin American Protestants? This is an even greater unexplored territory. There are lectures, books, sermons, and journals of the worthies of early Latin American Protestantism — preachers, bishops, missionary leaders. Here is a rich mine, barely opened up. Also, how have "simple believers" lived out their faith theologically? Where are the life stories, the spontaneous expressions in the face of death or in love or in daily life? How to discover these "mentalities"? All this is sufficiently fluid to allow one to venture into conjectures, to propose hypotheses, or to imagine scenarios without the possibility (and hence the responsibility) of supporting them academically. I offer no more than this.

In Latin America the word *evangélico* (or "evangelista," as "evangélicos" are sometimes called) covers both "Protestant" and "evangelical." Some forty years ago our beloved Adam F. Sosa questioned this identification and maintained that our churches were in truth "evangelical" and not Protestant. My reaction to this thesis was negative and I attempted to demonstrate a firm Protestant rootage — "heirs of the reformation of Luther and Calvin" — of the Latin American Protestant churches. I still adhere to that thesis but must admit that, with regard to most of our churches, the heritage has been reshaped in other lands and with other molds, and ignorance of these mediation processes has been a grave obstacle for us to understand ourselves as Protestants. This book, in part, is an effort of reflection on this "transference."

Precisely here I came upon my greatest frustration in these lectures. I decided to circumscribe the topic to "three faces" of Latin American Protestantism — liberal, evangelical, and Pentecostal — deliberately excluding what has been variously called "immigration Protestantism," "transplanted churches," or "ethnic churches." My reasons, which I deemed sufficient, partly were that such a subject required a different focus and methodology. Basically I did not have — and still lack — the historical knowledge in this field, nor do we have sufficient research, to enable us to speak with certainty on this point. It did not occur to me that this exclusion might negate the importance and significance of these churches, and still less that I might fail to consider them as an authentic manifestation of Latin American Protestantism. The clearly indignant reaction of many pastors of those churches — dear fellow students, personal friends with whom we share with complete frankness, colleagues in the ministry and in the academic world with whom we work in all kinds of daily common tasks — proved to me that I had not realized what I had done. My decision, which I took to be merely functional and "economic," could only be understood as taking a position. More profoundly, it demonstrated that, even if I felt profoundly in my heart and my experience that we "belong together" as Christians and Protestant churches, *I did not know how to express that sentiment and that experience in theological and historical terms.* Therefore, I decided to include a new chapter, not because I have discovered a response, but because we cannot be content not to attempt it; it will be a chapter of mutual questionings, maybe irritating, open questions, and perhaps some proposals. All this — at least for me — beneath an overarching conviction that Jesus Christ has already constituted us all as a singular subject of faith, and that his Spirit has revealed and continues to reveal to us the way and the tasks which we have already begun to undertake.

The image evoked by the title I have chosen is ambiguous: Are there different "faces" because there are different subjects? Or are they "masks" of a single subject? If so, how is the face hidden behind these masks? The search for an answer has led me to seek a hermeneutical key which would allow the recognition of a unique identity, the true diversity, and the coexistence of that identity within each manifestation of that subject, which is Latin American Protestantism. This is the intent of the theological exploration of the two final chapters. The trinitarian analogy must not be sought, in any case, in some direct or attributive manner — that would be the worst error — but in the unity of intention and purpose, in the communion of love. What this means in terms of forms and expressions — doctrinal, institutional, missionary, testimonial, cultural — of that unity is a task that we Latin American Protestants still have before us.

Two observations to complete this presentation and *apologia pro liber meu*. Rereading the text I note that at times the tone moves beyond argument and analysis to rhetoric and exhortation. I do not apologize for that. What good are arguments and analyses if they do not aim to convince, if they are not at the service of a passion? However, I do not wish to be interpreted as one who has definitive answers but as one who invites readers to a common reflection and a joint passion in relation to this promise and pain which is Latin American Protestantism. It is also at the service of this invitation that I have allowed myself a perhaps excessive number of reference notes and open questions to encourage the kind of dialogue that I believe our Protestantism needs.

It is proper at this juncture of a preface to include words of gratitude. Those who deserve my thanks include an interminable list of colleagues, friends, brothers and sisters in the faith throughout the length and breadth of our continent and in other lands. I cannot, nor do I wish to, leave unmentioned the three interlocutors and friends who accompanied me in these lectures and in the morning seminars, Professors Elsa Tamez, Antonio Gouvea Mendonça, and Bernardo Campos, whose comments, information, and criticisms helped me to deepen, amplify, and correct the original text; undoubtedly many features of the original outline of the "faces" gained precision thanks to their help. I am especially thankful to my three sons who, often at the family table when grandchildren allowed, provided me with information and historical, sociological, and biblical references I would be unable to gather by myself. The forty-eight years during which I have enjoyed the patience and impatience of Noemí, my wife, exceed the possibility of any adequate words of gratitude.

1. The Liberal Face of Protestantism in Latin America

PROTESTANT CHRISTIANITY in Latin America? Why and how? Let us begin with some opinions and judgments:

> [Protestantism is] a form of North American capitalism, a "conquistador" element, a friend of the capitalist and enemy of the worker, created through its schools, its temples and its sports, the Americanization of the people.[1]

> Therefore, Latin American Protestantism was established here in the "womb" of a foreign invasion, and it bears the marks of the sectarianism and individualism that characterized it. It turned out to be, thus, an acculturation that has nothing to do with our origin and historical development, and it is a subproduct of political, economic, and cultural conquests of past centuries.[2]

> I firmly believe that to extend the Reformation to the Latin American world in an intelligent and vigorous way is to provoke the struggles of conscience in which the strong characters so necessary for the

---

1. Regis Planchet, *La intervención protestante en México y Sudamérica; Revista Católica* (El Paso, Texas, 1928), p. 180; see also, by the same author, *La propaganda del Protestantismo en México, Revista Católica* (El Paso, 1922); cf. Camilo Crivelli, *Los Protestantes y la América Latina* (Isola de Liri: Maccioce y Pisani, 1931), pp. 104-7.
2. Waldo Cesar et al., *Protestantismo e Imperialismo no America Latina* (Petropolis: Vozes, 1968), p. 12.

1

aggrandizement and the salvation of the republics are forged and tempered; it is to take [to the Latin American people] the vivifying breath of the freedoms thus conquered by the peoples of the North.[3]

The Catholic debater, the "repentant" Protestant of the 1960s, and the enthusiastic evangelical intellectual of 1916 present very different evaluations. They seem to coincide, however, in the recognition of a historical and ideological relationship among Latin American Protestantism, the liberal modernizing systems of Latin American political sectors, and North American influence. Any unprejudiced observer would probably have to concede, at least in chronological terms, the credibility of this relationship. With some precisions that I shall eventually point out, the second half of the last century is the historical locus where these three processes converge in Latin America — the liberal system, the predominance of the United States, and the entrance of Protestantism. What relationship links them? What are the characteristics of each of these factors? And how should this period be evaluated historically, ideologically, and theologically? These questions have been the object of passionate discussions and have to do with the self-consciousness and identity of Latin American Protestantism. My contribution to this discussion is limited in this context to posing three questions: (1) If there is a relationship, what is its historical importance? (2) Where lies the "affinity" that might have made this relationship possible? (3) How do we Protestants respond to this "presumed" historical past in terms of our mission here and now?

I. Does This Relationship Exist, and What Is Its Importance?

We shall not be distracted by the analysis of what is designated — and discarded — by Jean-Pierre Bastian as the "conspiration thesis."[4] Ac-

---

3. Erasmo Braga, *Panamericanismo: aspecto Religioso* (New York: Sociedad para la Educación Misionera en los Estados Unidos y el Canadá, 1917), pp. 199ff.; Spanish version by E. Monteverde.

4. Jean-Pierre Bastian, *Historia del Protestantismo en América Latina* (Mexico City: Casa Unida de Publicaciones S.A., 1990), pp. 178ff. The different lines of argument are repeated whenever circumstances appear that "threaten" a modification of the religious field. In this regard, of interest is the research of Alejandro Frigerio, "The Invasion of the Sects: The Debate about New Religious Movements in the Communications Media in Argentina," *Sociedad y Religión*, no. 10/11 (June 1993): 24-51.

cording to this thesis (as shown by our first quote), Protestant missions were nothing other than the "spearhead," "the ideological accompaniment," or "the religious legitimation" of the economic, political, and cultural penetration of the United States into Latin America — in any case a conscious and deliberate instrument of the neocolonial project. It is a theory often set forth by Roman Catholic apologists, at times allied to right-wing nationalists, and later by some Marxists, a theory, moreover, which has disturbed the conscience of not a few "progressive" Protestants in the 1960s, leading at times to premature repudiations and "confessions."

Apart from coincidences in time, very few items of evidence back up this theory. For one thing, one would have to be precise about dates, since United States imperialism only took shape in Latin America after the Civil War in that country (1860), while the Protestant presence had already been in Latin America for more than two decades. In any case, the opening up of the religious panorama of the continent is rather to be attributed (for good or ill) to British influence and pressure since the wars of independence.

Very different, and in my opinion far better founded, is the "associative hypothesis" Bastian himself formulates in these terms:

> Therefore the raison d'etre of Protestant societies in Latin America during these decades had less to do with "North American imperialism" than with the internal political and social struggles in the continent, which can be summarized as the confrontation between an authoritarian political culture and the minorities that sought to found a bourgeois modernity based on the individual redeemed from his caste origin and hence on the equality of a participatory and representative democracy, hoping thereby to put an end to multisecular privileges.[5]

To be sure, this thesis does not keep Bastian from recognizing that "the systematic emergence of Protestantisms beginning in the second half of the nineteenth century finds its explanation in the expansion of the capitalist production model on a continental scale,"[6] nor that, especially toward 1916, the missionary movement adopts the slogan of "panamericanism" and thus "a difficult road was opened up" by which "Prot-

5. Bastian, p. 187.
6. Ibid., p. 22.

estantism was entangled with the North American ideological penetration in the continent."[7]

The value of Bastian's hypothesis resides in the recognition that the entrance of Protestantism is basically explained by a situation endogenous to Latin America (the struggle for liberal modernization), and it is there that Protestantism allies itself with Latin American sectors that impel that process, principally, in his view, with "liberation associations" of various kinds (Masonic lodges, laborers' associations, groups of intellectuals, parapolitical societies).

If in principle we accept this hypothesis (we shall make some critical observations), several questions arise. First, who are the Protestants that take on this "association"? Recent studies seem to indicate that, at least until the end of the nineteenth century — the most important period for this subject — they included some of the missionaries related to the more "liberal" churches (Methodists, Presbyterians, and some Baptists), as well as some "intellectuals" (some of them dissident ex-priests) who early on joined Protestantism. What is curious is that — as we shall see — these missionaries had a conservative and pietistic spiritual and theological formation that ill correlates with the secularist orientation of some of their more radicalized Latin American "partners." One may suppose that the "association" occurred on the basis of a coincidence in the affirmation of a democratic society — the North American model of which attracted all of them — and, probably even more, was due to the missionary need to secure an opening for the freedom of conscience and worship. Latin American leaders, in turn, found in this alliance a support for their struggle against clerical opposition to the reforms they wished to introduce. I do not think it exaggerated to suspect that here we have a convergence of interests more than a similarity of ideas. We shall return to this topic in the next chapter. In any case, it has to do with the "elites" in each group, for as regards the new converts that entered Protestantism from the marginal sectors of society (apart from its repercussions in the area of religious liberty) the "association" had very little importance.

There is, nevertheless, a second consideration. I have not found statistics of the Latin American Protestant population around 1840, but the references and available data lead us to believe there were only a few thousand, most of them foreigners or a result of very limited missionary

7. Ibid., p. 160.

work, practically limited to Bible distribution and mission "efforts" (Argentina, Brazil) which were often frustrated. The major impact of the nineteenth century takes place in the second half of the century, with the conditions opened up by the triumphs of liberal sectors. Even so, the 1903 statistics are under 120,000.[8] It is occasionally said that the Protestant presence had far greater weight than its numbers. That may have been so. Yet it is curious that it is only Protestants who say that. A review of the historical works of the best-known "secular" authors (both Latin American and English-language authors) shows an almost total absence of references to the Protestant presence. Even those who discuss the religious reality of the time and the struggle for religious tolerance, such as Halperin Donghi or the North American Burns, do not assign Protestantism any role as the "subject" of these processes. John Lynch's conclusion is lapidary: "Yet, even after a century of growth, Protestantism was a rare and exotic phenomenon in Latin America. In the struggle for minds, the Catholic faith had a more potent rival" — Positivism.[9] Shall we attribute this void only to "prejudices" shared by such diverse authors? Might it not be, rather, that challenged by the need to "enter history" and to vindicate their Latin American legitimacy, some early Protestant historians and intellectuals have "inflated" limited and circumstantial participation and actions or the recognition provided by Latin American notables (Sarmiento, Alberdi, Juárez, Bello, etc.), often using quotations that appear selective and decontextualized when seen in the light of their complete works? Words which we have transformed into a hermeneutical key to understand a history in which our presence has in truth been marginal.

Ironically, this vindication was to return as a condemnation in the face of the model to which it was linked, thus setting in motion feelings of unease, guilt, and self-repudiation in a subsequent generation.

8. The figure given for 1903 comes from Joseph I. Parker, ed., *Interpretative Statistical Survey of the World Mission of the Christian Church* (New York and London: International Missionary Council, 1938), less the corresponding figure for the non-Hispanic Caribbean.

9. John Lynch, "The Catholic Church," in *Latin America Economy and Society,* ed. Leslie Bethell (Cambridge: Cambridge University Press, 1989), pp. 331-36, esp. the summary on p. 332 cited in the text.

II. What Liberal Project?

The most recent Protestant historiography coincides in locating in the Panama Protestant Congress of 1916 a decisive moment in the self-consciousness of Latin American Protestantism. With two caveats, I agree with this interpretation. First, it was largely a "missionary" congress; in that regard it helps us delineate the concept and strategy of the missionary enterprise, which must not be uncritically identified with the daily life, the piety, and the practice of the Protestant congregations in the continent. Second, it was a congress controlled by the historic "liberal" denominations (I use the term "liberal" in the North American meaning of "progressive" or "advanced") of the United States: Methodists, Presbyterians, Disciples of Christ, the American Baptist Convention (of the North), and even more, by the "liberal" missionary sectors of these denominations. There was no presence, or at least no decisive influence, of British missions or of the missions of the Southern Baptist Convention, the Christian and Missionary Alliance, the Church of the Nazarene, or the Plymouth Brethren, who already were present in Latin America and who would play a very important role in a subsequent period.

All in all, Panama is important for our study. It condenses a reflection of the North American missions which, since the Edinburgh Missionary Conference of 1910 (where Latin American missions were excluded), was developing into an organic whole. It sets in motion a series of initiatives, particularly the Committee on Cooperation in Latin America (CCLA), as a permanent organism of coordination, with programs of consultation and publication, which bore fruit in regional councils and federations and in diverse means of cooperation. Hence it is well to stop for a moment to locate Panama 1916 against its historical, ecclesiastical, and theological background.

A. The United States and Latin America from the Mid–Nineteenth Century

In 1823 President Monroe defined his Doctrine, summarized as "America for the Americans," after many hesitations and presumably as a protection against the risk that the consolidated Europe of the 1814 Restoration might seek to gain positions in Latin America. Surely, nevertheless, the Doctrine has a wider significance: the vindication of Latin America as a security zone, for political control and commercial hegemony, of the United States. For such reasons, undoubtedly, the British initiative of making that protective declaration a joint one was rejected. The consequences did not become immediately evident; concentration on the conquest of the West as well as internal crises, the concern to consolidate territorial control, and "the conquest of the seas" (Mahan) were of primary focus. Toward the middle of the century, however, the old slogan of "manifest destiny"[10] was interpreted as a criterion in the relationship with southern neighbors. Once the annexation of Florida and Louisiana was completed, the control of the Caribbean (particularly Cuba and Puerto Rico) appears to have been the immediate goal. The strategies to incorporate Texas, New Mexico, and Lower California — already explicit following the 1820 decade — range from the offer to purchase to the deliberate insertion of populations and finally to war in 1845.

Economic penetration was slower. Toward the end of the century Great Britain still maintained economic and commercial hegemony in most of the Latin American nations. Changes, nevertheless, continued to favor the United States. Already at the end of the colonial period the mercantile model was losing ground in Latin America. For some time the winds of emancipation revolutions blew in favor of mercantilism by legalizing and amplifying the diversified mercantile relationships that already existed, mainly with Great Britain and France. The Creole elites that predominated in the first decades of the century were only intent on transferring the commercial monopoly, religious patronage, and social structures characteristic of colonial times to their own benefit. For a time they achieved this without major difficulty, but soon it became evident that the mercantile model was exhausted and it was necessary to advance toward a production model. That involved incorporating a new work force into the economic system, which meant the stimulation of immigration and the education of the people. All this demanded also a transformation of minds, new habits, and values: in

10. The theme of "manifest destiny" has a long history in the culture and politics of the United States, not unrelated to messianic conceptions and to theological influences. Two works that well summarize and interpret this history are Albert K. Weinberg, *Manifest Destiny: A Study of Nationalist Expansionism in American History* (Baltimore: Johns Hopkins Press, 1935), and Frederick Merk, *Manifest Destiny and Mission in American History: A Reinterpretation* (New York, 1963).

brief, the entrance to enlightened "modernity."[11] At this point, the liberal trends came up against the resistance of a Catholic Vatican that had taken up the banner of struggle against liberal modernity and little by little was recovering control of the disorganized Latin American church, which had been left adrift after the struggles for independence. The new elite that began to gather power — in lengthy and complex struggles — from the mid–nineteenth century onward represented this new vision. Their democratic and progressive dreams and their economic necessities led them toward the North American model and, even if they maintained some reservations similar to their predecessors, they "naturally gravitated" in that direction — as already John Quincy Adams predicted in 1823.[12] The economic absorption of Central America occurred already in the last decades of the century; the hegemony in Brazil and the northern countries of South America grew from the century's end, and the rest only after the Great War (1914-18).

The "conquistador" profile of the "panamerican" politics of the United States aroused, as we know, varying reactions among the governing elites of Latin America. Some governments wanted to maintain "European" relationships as a containment brake; others proposed a kind of Bolivarian "panamericanism." Most, sincerely or not, opposed armed interventions. Toward 1880 the United States began to redefine its policies in terms of "panamericanism" and in 1888 invited all Latin American nations to Washington for the First International Conference of American States. Gordon Connell-Smith summarizes the problem of interpretation in a pair of memorable phrases:

> It has been a sedulously cultivated myth that the inter American system, which was formally established as a result of the Washington Conference, is based upon the ideals of Simon Bolivar: that Bolivar is the father of Pan Americanism. Such a myth clearly serves the interests of those in the United States — and Latin America — anxious to promote Pan Americanism. It has no basis in reality — except that myths create their own reality.[13]

---

11. We shall return to the topic of the search by the liberal Latin American leadership for an immigration that would contribute to the new model in chapter 4.

12. Quoted in Gordon Connell-Smith, *The United States and Latin America: An Historical Analysis of Inter-American Relations* (New York: John Wiley and Sons, 1974), pp. 60ff.

13. Ibid., p. 108.

A different understanding of "panamericanism" had dominated the continental congresses of Panama 1825, Lima 1847, Santiago de Chile 1856, and the Second Lima Congress of 1865, in all of which the United States had been absent, and which precisely understood themselves as attempts to build defenses against the North American advance as well as the European menace. The tension between these two conceptions was evident in the 1888 conference. The opposition of several governments (particularly that of Argentina) frustrated various North American proposals (for example, that of a unified customs system) and at the same time the United States veto rejected resolutions contrary to the "right of conquest" or the "Calvo clause" that would have impeded foreigners from appealing to laws other than those of the countries where they resided . . . and conducted business. Later conduct of the United States under Theodore Roosevelt (1901-9), William Taft (1909-13), and even Woodrow Wilson (1913-21) only confirmed Latin American fears. This last reference is important because Wilson's statements attempt a "liberal" definition of panamericanism:

> [In this hemisphere] the future . . . is going to be very different from the past. . . . the Latin American states . . . have had harder bargains driven with them in the matter of loans than any other peoples in the world. . . . I rejoice in nothing so much as in the prospect that they will now be emancipated from these conditions, and we ought to be the first to take part in assisting in that emancipation. . . . We must show ourselves friends by comprehending their interests whether it squares with our own interest or not.[14]

Yet when the same Wilson argues that

> since trade ignores national boundaries and the manufacturer insists on having the world as a market, the flag of his nation must follow him, and the doors of the nations which are closed against him must be battered down. Concessions obtained by financiers must be safeguarded by ministers of state, even if the sovereignty of unwilling nations be outraged in the process. Colonies must be obtained or planted, in order that no useful concern of the world may be overlooked or left unused. . . .

14. Ibid., pp. 60f. México, Fondo de Cultura Económica, 1974, pp. 84-85.

and, uniting action to words, intervenes, exercising political pressure, in the internal politics of Mexico and carries out armed interventions in the Caribbean (Dominican Republic, Nicaragua, and Haiti), one can understand the conclusion reached by the North American historian van Alstyne about a "strong smell of Phariseeism in North American diplomacy."[15]

B. We Are Now in 1916

In Latin America the "Latin American" interpretation of the (Protestant) Panama Congress appears in print in Portuguese by the distinguished Brazilian educator, Erasmo Braga, and in Spanish by the Uruguayan Eduardo Monteverde (the official documents are only in English) with the title: "Panamericanism, Its Religious Aspect." Naivete? Deliberate complicity? Genuine conviction? Probably all of these and at the same time none of these. To the (limited) degree that Latin American Protestantism in this period is formulated and represented by the Panama Congress, it is clear that there was an explicit alliance with "panamericanism." But which panamericanism? That of Wilson's statements or that of his actions? That of the Washington Conference or that of the "continental congresses"? It is also clear that the leaders gathered in Panama saw the future of Latin American nations as a "liberal project." But which liberal project? Referring to the progressive governments of the second half of the nineteenth century, Halperin classified these projects as liberal (Mexico, the River Plate, Uruguay), Cesaro-progressive (Venezuela, Guatemala, Central America, Ecuador), and oligarchic (Colombia, Peru, Chile), plus Brazil.[16] It is evident that the neocolonial question was understood and carried out in many diverse ways. What does the Panama Congress represent in the midst of this diversity?

I cannot stop here for a detailed study of the history, contents, and results of the event. There is a vast bibliography in which one can

15. R. W. van Alstyne, *The Rising American Empire* (New York: Oxford University Press, 1960), p. 7.

16. See Tulio Halperin Donghi, *Historia Contemporánea de América Latina* (Buenos Aires: Alianza Editorial, 1986), pp. 189-250; ET, *The Contemporary History of Latin America* (Durham, N.C.: Duke University Press, 1933).

discover the various interpretations.[17] It is, I believe, an ambiguous event, in which there were differences, divergences, and contradictions. However, if we pay attention to the voices of those who evidently led the preparatory process and had a decisive role in the development of the congress and the implementation of its resolutions, it is possible to discover a quite homogeneous vision of the *enlightened Protestantism* that motivated them.

As for "panamericanism," it is scarcely necessary to document the Panama Congress's rejection of armed "interventionism." Indeed, several missionaries had already condemned it explicitly in relation to the war with Mexico and the interventions in Central America, and they had denounced the economic interests hidden behind them. Ten years later, a conservative missionary — Susan Strachan — spoke, with regard to the Coolidge administration and its conflicts with the Mexican government, of the "heroic" effort of Mexican President Calles, who "deserved the prayers and the sympathy of all true Christians in his gigantic struggle." She added: "He faced two insatiable enemies, one the church of Rome and the other the rival foreign business enterprises that had caused the political upsets in Mexico for the last two decades."[18] All this, however, is for them only an excrescence of a cultural, political, and economic relationship that should be open, generous, and fruitful for both "Americas." One of the sections of the Panama report recognizes that

> the offending have been aggressive commercial agents, the plundering type of concessionaires, overbearing, arrogant industrial managers and bosses, swaggering tourists, ill-bred consular and diplomatic representatives, and occasionally, condescending missionaries.[19]

However, they state that the majority of the North American people are not like that. The report, citing the author García Calderón,

---

17. A wide bibliography is available in the histories of Hans-Jürgen Prien, Jean-Pierre Bastian, and Pablo A. Deiros.

18. Cited in the article of John Stam, "La Misión Latinoamericana y el imperialismo norteamericano," *Taller de Teología* 9 (Mexico City, 1981): 52. The entire article is extremely interesting, given its historical moment, the growth of fundamentalism in the United States and its nationalist political guise, and the character of the Latin American Mission at that time.

19. Report No. 2, cited in Braga-Monteverde, p. 41.

urges a look rather at "the spectacle of that other America, disdainful of violent materialism and of the immoral greed of practical men."[20] Hence it insists on the need for greater mutual knowledge and a relationship that destroys prejudices and does away with "the suspicions that the new (panamericanist) doctrine harbors the seed of the predominance of the eagle of the North."[21] Nevertheless, the report does not hesitate to see, in the opening up of the Panama Canal or in the recently inaugurated Pan-American Railroad, auspicious signs that shine as a foretaste of this new relationship and do not seem to be sullied by "violent materialism" or "greed."

Citations could be multiplied that demonstrate, almost ad infinitum, that arising from this "ingenuousness," the work of CCLA and its operators in Latin America (persons such as Guy Inman, Stanley Rycroft, and others) places itself at the service of a growing relationship between the United States and Latin America — at missionary, educational, social, and economic levels. Precisely the unity and interconnection of these aspects are what characterize the version of panamericanism they promote. It is evident that the religious, educational, and social dimensions — especially in aid — predominate over the economic dimension, but do not separate themselves from it. They only attempt to "purify it," denouncing its corruptions, which they attribute to the moral defects of some of its agents and not to structural reasons implicit in the system or the ideology that inspires it.

Not all in North American Protestantism share this "ingenuousness." In an article published in 1929, Francis P. Miller, at the time president of the World Student Christian Federation, spoke of "the American [USA] invasion of the world" and linked it to the new economic "rationality" that took control of the totality of the life of the North American nation. A brief quotation summarizes his analysis and concern:

> Whatever the future may have in store for us, the fact remains that the national framework at the moment is a framework of production and merchandising. It is the machine of American industry and commerce which gives us national cohesion. The system and the technique which that machine has called into being are the most dynamic forces

20. Ibid., p. 19.
21. Ibid., p. 18.

of our national life. Far more than any of us are aware, these forces are changing our mentality as individuals and our customs as a society. . . . Such, in brief, is the picture of the United States seen by the nations which feel the full impact of her economic invasion.[22]

The influence of these ideas would not be felt in Latin American Protestantism until two or three decades later, but the impact of the Social Gospel, united to the anti-imperialist concerns introduced by socialists and anarchists into the Latin America political discussions, awakened in some Latin American Protestant leaders a certain questioning of the "panamericanist" emphasis of CCLA. We shall return to this point in section III.

C. Incoherences

In my interpretation, the incoherences noticeable in Panama — which would turn into open contradictions in Montevideo 1925 and Havana 1929 — arise from two sources. One is theological and has to do with a twofold influence in the academic formation and the spiritual orientation of leadership groups. It is true, as Bastian says, that many missionary leaders studied in the liberal universities of New England and the Ivy League (Harvard, Yale, Columbia, Princeton) and there absorbed elements of progressive liberal ideologies, which in part they interpreted theologically with the Social Gospel that emerged in their churches from the beginning of the century. On the other hand, the missionary movement they joined was strongly marked by the "second awakening," with its individualistic and subjective soteriology: the person of John R. Mott, perhaps the most important symbolic figure in the entire movement, is the most complete illustration of this "conservatively progressive" posture. If the liberal vision led them to design a socially committed missionary model, missionary soteriology obliged them at once to down-

22. Francis P. Miller, *Americanism and Christianity* (New York: National Council of YMCA, Student Division, 1929), p. 7. The reflection of this statement by Professor Miller is mainly directed at the relationship with Europe and the efforts of the World Student Christian Federation (WSCF) to redefine the theological basis and guidelines of a social reconstruction on the basis of personal responsibility and participatory democracy. One notes at once the synthesis of Social Gospel ideas, participatory democracy, and the new theological concerns that began to appear in Europe.

play it. The debate generated in Panama on the Report of the Message Committee, which led to a correction of the slightly liberal and progressive theological tone of the committee's proposal, illustrates this tension, to which we will allude in the next chapter.[23]

The second reason for the incoherence stems from the superposition of two democratic models debated at the time among North American political theorists. C. B. Macpherson has characterized them very well, distinguishing the two "liberal" visions: "democracy as protection" and "democracy as development." The first begins by accepting as a presupposition a capitalist society ruled by the market and hence by a certain conception of human beings and society. To wit, the human being as a "maximizer of utilities" is defined as the one who is the most rationally efficient, that is to say, who obtains the greatest profit with the largest economy of effort. Society is only a sum of individuals with conflicting interests, since each one pursues this "maximization," inevitably in some measure, to the detriment of others. The philosophic formulation of this vision was utilitarianism, expressed by Jeremy Bentham as "the calculation of happiness" — the greatest happiness for the greatest number. Nevertheless, how to measure happiness? Since a quantitative measure is necessary, what appears at once is money: "Money is the instrument with which one measures the amount of pain or pleasure" (Bentham). What then might be the function of the state, laws, and government, other than the protection of the fairness of this social process? To that end, the state must insure the free, unimpeded functioning of the market, which in turn will guarantee, in the competitive struggle, subsistence, abundance, equality, and security for all. The government is the "referee" that does not allow "low blows." The vote, secret, universal, and frequent, is the adequate and sufficient instrument that assures that the state will fulfill this role. (At first Bentham as well as James Mill thought of a limited or qualified suffrage, but later they were convinced that the problems that would entail were such that it was preferable to have universal suffrage.)

23. Though we do not have many adequate biographical studies about the early missionaries, the few we have seem to coincide in this profile; cf., only as illustrations, Irven Paul, *A Yankee Reformer in Chile: The Life and Works of David Trunbull* (South Pasadena, Calif.: William Carey Library, 1973); G. Stuart McIntosh, *The Life and Times of John Ritchie, 1878-1952* (Lima, Peru: MAC Research Monographs, 1988); John H. Sinclair, *Juan A. Mackay un escocés con alma latina* (Mexico City: Casa Unida de Publicaciones, 1990).

From the middle of the nineteenth century, however — and this is important for our study — a new democratic vision appears. The working class makes its weight felt, as much by the spectacle of its misery as by the power of its protest. John Stuart Mill states his critique thus:

> I confess that I am not charmed with the ideal of life held out by those who think that the normal state of human life is that of struggling to get on; that the trampling, crushing, elbowing, and treading on each other's heels, which form the existing type of social life, are the most desirable lot of human kind or anything but the disagreeable symptoms of one of the phases of industrial progress.[24]

As a result, a new generation of intellectuals — John Stuart Mill, John Dewey, Robert M. McIver — poses a different conception. The human being is one who tries to achieve betterment as a moral being and does not solely want to accumulate, but also seeks development. Society, in turn, is in a process of searching for greater freedom and equality. Thus, the goal is "the advancement of the community in terms of intellect, virtue, practical activity and efficiency" (John Stuart Mill). From this vantage point, John Stuart critiques his father James's model but does not reject capitalism. How then to advance toward a different society? For him it is a difficult question: He proposes qualifications of the vote, which would assure a greater distribution of resources (a curious anticipation of "affirmative action"!), the creation of cooperatives, and representative political parties. McIver makes a sharp distinction between state and community and tries to give to the latter a greater protagonism in the orientation of society. John Dewey adds a decisive contribution: *Education is the way.* The object is to "develop a better generation." That is the idea that predominates in Panama 1916.

D. The Missionary Educational Project

One need not be very insightful to note that here, far more than at the political and social level, liberal missionary Protestantism finds a possibility for integrating its various strands. It responds to a Protestant tradition that goes back to the Reformation and has been basic in North

---

24. *Principles of Political Economy*, bk. 4, chap. 6, sec. 2; in *Works*, iii:754-55.

American Protestantism — the emphasis on education and the creation of schools. It offers an unobjectionable mediation toward what is social without having to take a stand on political regimes or economic matters. It permits reconciliation of the "conversionist" emphasis with ethical concern and the liberal notion of personal development — "an education that builds character" is a motto that recurs in the Protestant educational programs throughout the continent — and offers a wide field of cooperation with the new enlightened elites of Latin America, who are themselves obsessed with "redeeming the people" through education. The two streams leading to the theme of education delineated in the missionary project are magnificently illustrated in the discussions registered in volume one of the Panama report.[25] On the one hand are those who see the mission of education as a way toward religious decision; on the other, those who hope for conversion as a development of "integral" growth of the student in contact with the education of a Protestant school. Both coincide, however — at least at this stage of Protestant history in the continent — in seeing that the various purposes of "missionary cooperation" are fulfilled in the redemption of the people and the building of a new future for Latin American nations. Jether Ramalho Pereira has summed up well — referring to Brazil — the inspiration of the Protestant educational purpose in all of Latin America:

> The central proposition of this work [his research] is to demonstrate that the principles and characteristics of the educational practices introduced in Brazil at the end of the last century and in the first decades of this century, by schools coming from the historic denominations of Protestantism, of North American origin, only can be understood insofar as they are related to the ideological version that inspires them most profoundly and gives them meaning, and to the structural conditions of the new society in which they will be engaged.[26]

25. *Christian Work in Latin America* (New York: Missionary Education Movement, 1917), vol. 1.

26. Jether Ramalho Pereira, *Pratica Educativa e Sociedade* (Rio de Janeiro: Zahar, 1975), p. 10. This work is a careful study of Brazilian schools in the historical context of Brazil and of the ideological guidelines that influenced this educational project.

III. To Renounce the Liberal Heritage?

A. Failure of the "Liberal Project"

Rubem Alves called it Protestantism's "utopian project" in Latin America and described its wreck as "Protestantism of correct doctrine."[27] "Utopian" may here have the positive significance of a liberating "Protestant principle" which — as already Tillich had said — was incapable of opening up a way to Western culture beyond the crisis of the Great War. It may also be read negatively: an expectation without foundation in reality, destined to collide with reality. In the first sense — as it was read by the Latin American Protestant apologists — we have suggested that its historical gains were of little significance.

Probably one has to conclude that, as a specific historical project for Latin American Protestantism since the mid–nineteenth century, and for more than a century, the project failed. With a retrospective glance — which always has the wisdom of irreversible facts — it is possible to see that the failure was inevitable. On the one hand, it was due to the ambiguity of a theological position that did not allow the missionary leadership, as a whole, to integrate this project into its theological self-understanding. It was also due to an insufficient analysis that did not foresee the incompatibility of the "democracy as human development" project with the economic and political rationale that dictated the functioning of United States "panamericanism." On the other hand, it did not penetrate beyond small groups of the church's own membership, and even less did it reach the waves of holiness and fundamentalist churches that entered Latin America at the end of the century. These holiness and fundamentalistic churches influenced, in various degrees, all of Latin American Protestantism. And finally — and very importantly — because the project itself was not viable in Latin America, the very elites that sponsored it stumbled on impossibilities due to the social structure and to their own ambivalence, and ended up defeated or absorbed by the dependent capitalist model.

Perhaps the first indications of the crisis were felt around 1930, and they are important for our subject. In effect, the crisis of world

27. Rubem Alves, "Función ideológica y posibilidades utópicas del protestantismo latinoamericano," in *De la Iglesia y la Sociedad* (Montevideo: Tierra Nueva, 1971), pp. 4ff. See also, by the same author, *Protestantism and Repression: A Brazilian Case Study* (Maryknoll, N.Y.: Orbis, 1985).

capitalism in 1929 had decisive consequences for the social, economic, and political life of Latin America. The economic recession expelled millions of rural inhabitants who sought a space in cities or in the new mining and industrial centers. Unemployment, social anomie, and the poverty of the masses awakened social protest and opened wide the doors to socialist movements. The political response of the system was "populism": the effort to generate social change by means of an "alliance" of popular sectors and cultural and economic Latin American elites, within the structures of the capitalist system.

The more traditional Protestant current, still under the tutelage of the missionary movement, tried to find its identity and define its mission in this new situation, as Bastian puts it, as "a way of humanization that would recover the fundamental values in a society that has lost its orientation."[28] "Political independence," wrote W. Stanley Rycroft, the distinguished Presbyterian missionary, "did not bring freedom to the people, in the real sense of the word. That freedom has still to be gained, and is bound up intimately with the spread of Protestant Christianity."[29] That optimistic vision was repeated in the writing of some of the young Latin American Protestant leaders: for example, the Mexicans Alberto Rembao and Gonzalo Báez Camargo, the Brazilian Erasmo Braga, the Argentine-American Jorge P. Howard, and missionaries such as Samuel Guy Inman and John A. Mackay. Between the brutality of an insensitive capitalism and the materialism of a communism that preached class struggle, these leaders saw Protestantism as the avant-garde of true democracy, socially progressive, modernizing, and participatory, such as described in the previous section. The emphasis of the Social Gospel on social redemption and of Protestants on personal transformation seemed thus to find their unity.

---

28. Bastian, p. 189.

29. W. Stanley Rycroft, *On This Foundation* (New York: Friendship Press, 1942), p. 186. At almost the same time Jorge P. Howard published his book, *La Libertad Religiosa en América Latina* (Buenos Aires: La Aurora, 1945), a survey designed to show, with testimonies of Latin American intellectual and political leaders, Protestantism's contribution to democratic life in Latin America, thus countering an antimissionary campaign of the Catholic church. The same publishers, La Aurora and Casa Unida de Publicaciones (related to CCLA), published about those same years (1949-51) the Spanish translation of Federico Hoffet's book, *Imperialismo Protestante*, a vibrant apologia of the progressive role of Protestantism, at the world level, in the construction of advanced, progressive, and successful democracies, as compared to the backwardness of countries where Roman Catholicism was dominant.

Along these lines, from the 1930s to the 1950s, "councils" or "federations" of churches were created in most countries of the continent. The declared objectives were cooperation in literature publication, joint representation before public authorities, defense of religious liberty, and cooperation in evangelization and Christian education. The dominant theology and ideologies were those described above. A vigorous publications program spread translations of some ancient and modern classics of Protestant theology. Interdenominational seminaries were founded in Cuba, Argentina, and Puerto Rico, and denominational seminaries in other countries were renovated, nurturing a generation of Latin American leadership with an ecumenical mentality and a social concern that would emerge in the 1950s and 1960s. The first Latin American Protestant Conference convened and oriented from within Latin America (Conferencia Evangélica Latinoamericana — CELA I) met in Buenos Aires in 1949.

This Protestantism had no lack of leaders who stepped forward with a decided critique of the bourgeois capitalist model, and with an explicit sympathy for democratic socialism. Mackay himself criticized a report of the International Missionary Council "which reproduces the desires and interests of Western bourgeois society that sees Christianity as the heart of its culture but not its judge."[30] This critical attitude appears in the youth ecumenical movements that merged as the Union of Protestant Youth Leagues (Unión de Ligas Juveniles Evangélicas — ULAJE) in 1941, whose first congress had as its theme, "With Christ, a new world," called for a struggle against "the present capitalist system based on oppression and economic inequality," and favored "a system of cooperation." Similar options appear in the 1930 and 1940 documents of assemblies of the Methodist church in Chile, Uruguay, and Argentina. In the 1940s, "Christian student movements" appear, inspired by the World Student Christian Federation, oriented mainly from France along the same lines, which later, along with participation in the postwar ecumenical movement and on the basis of a more European theology, would generate the new leadership of the 1950s and 1960s.

30. See John A. Mackay, "The function of Christianity in relation to such a cultural effort [modern bourgeois society] is not that of providing a soul to perpetuate it but a reactive to produce a crisis"; "The Theology of the Laymen's Foreign Mission Report," *International Review of Missions* 22 (1933): 180.

Meanwhile, another wing of Protestantism, born in the late-nineteenth-century U.S. holiness movements, would follow a different course. In the next chapter we shall try to analyze this development and the tensions that came with the encounter. Now, however, we must take one more step in sketching the profile of the "liberal face." Everyone agrees in defining 1960 as a critical moment, which is variously characterized by Prien as "the crisis of the national oligarchic states," by Dussel as "the crisis of independent states" and "the crisis of liberation," and by Bastian as "the crisis of dependent capitalism: between resistance and submission." The promise of developmentalism, in which Protestantism — and a large part of the Latin American "enlightened world" — had rested its hope, vanished with the failure of Kennedy's Alliance for Progress and the CEPAL (Comisión Económica de las Naciones Unidas para América Latina) projects. It became clear that "utopian socialism," so present in the ULAJE documents — and in university movements tied to the "university reform" of 1918 — required more radical politics and a more solid ideological base. The famished face of the vast majorities becomes painfully visible in the misery belts that began to develop around the great capital cities. A new way of analysis was necessary to understand the dynamics of "peripheral" societies. The "[social-economic] dependence theory" set forth its own version of Marxist analysis, centered on the relation between developed/dependent worlds and the need for radical structural changes in the direction of a socialist project appropriate for Third World conditions.

In the religious world, awareness of this crisis echoed profoundly in Latin America. The theological and ecclesial renewal of Vatican II was read by the Medellin Episcopal Assembly in 1968 as a call for "the transformation of society," and the concern of the World Council of Churches for "nations on the way to development" became a call for "structural transformation" at the Geneva Conference in 1966, where the Latin American delegation played an important role. In Latin America, the Church and Society movement (Iglesia y Sociedad en América Latina — ISAL), born in 1960, raised the banner of structural change. The new leadership took up this view and based it on a biblical redemption theology of Barthian inspiration with a historical key, and called for active militancy in social and political liberation movements. In Protestantism, the names of Valdo Galland, Jorge César Mota, Richard Shaull, myself, Emilio Castro, and others represent a movement that opened up the way which Rubem Alves, Julio de Santa Ana, Gonzalo Castillo, Jether Ramalho Pereira, Raúl Macín, and others, in various ways and with varying shades, tried to deepen and develop. From the totality of these efforts — and analogous developments in Catholicism — was born, toward the end of the 1960s, the so-called liberation theology.[31]

B. What to Do with This Failure?

The 1960s generation clearly perceived the failure of the development model and, faced with the Gordian knot represented by the entwining of the humanist ideal with dependent capitalism, resorted to Alexander the Great's solution: it unsheathed the sword and cut the knot. Liberty, democracy, and development came to be pejorative terms; a unilateral interpretation of the "theology of crisis" and an equally partial application of Marxist analysis fed what I shall call, more modestly, the "strategy of rupture." Without doubt, psychological factors help us understand the harshness with which the rupture was manifested in some sectors of Protestantism (and also Catholicism). The awareness that the search for justice to which the human reality of the continent and the Christian faith had impelled them had been ideologically manipulated in a system of oppression precipitated personal crises, precisely among the most lucid and committed persons of this generation. The nucleus of this crisis, however, is found in the objective elements we have indicated. With "liberal Protestantism" discarded and "conservative Protestantism" unacceptable, an ecclesial and theological crisis, which we have not yet overcome, emerges in this Protestantism.

Is this the only possible response to the "failure" of the liberal project? For sectors of postmodernism, and ironically for reasons contrary to those of the 1960s generation, this seemed to be the only possibility. Gone is the era of "great stories" that charted the movement of history and inspired the utopia of progress; dead are the ideologies: we had reached the end of history. Here also Alexander's strategy is the only one suggested to solve the problem of the crisis of liberal modern-

---

31. I shall not here define the characteristics or analyze the development and the current state of liberation theology. The last two chapters of this book presume to take up central elements of that theology from a Protestant theological perspective. Perhaps, nonetheless, it is worth noting that the central intuitions of liberation theology are fully present in the thought and practice of faith in our historical and ecclesial context.

ity. It may well be even more painful to fall into the "mood" of hopeless cynicism that some 1960s "revolutionaries" have adopted in the face of the overwhelming and apparently invincible power of neoconservatism and of the "new international world order."

It is necessary to admit that the crisis of the development model and the installation of neoconservatism pose grave suspicions regarding any attempt to recover the "humanist heritage" that accompanied and frequently legitimized development projects. Questions must be asked, such as: Why does the "liberal" project allow itself to be absorbed so easily and place itself at the service of the interests of a few? Is it worth making the effort to identify and distinguish the "humanist" aspects of reformist programs and try to reintegrate them in terms of an "option for the poor"? Is there not an inherent contradiction in the total ideology of liberalism so that such a recuperation is impossible?[32] Was liberalism ever "democratic"?

There are, however, other equally urgent questions as well. Gustavo Gutiérrez once characterized liberation theology this way: "the goal is *freedom; liberation* is the way." If freedom is always — at least[33] historically — "a moving target" and liberation, also historically, is an endless road, do we have the right to separate one from the other? Or rather, is

32. The Peruvian sociologist and essayist Aníbal Quijano has discussed this topic in terms of the so-called crisis of modernity which appears when "[its] original promises of the liberation of society and of each of its members from the social inequities and the hierarchies based on them" seem to be denied and contradicted by the very history of modernity. In his *Modernidad, identidad y utopía en América Latina* (Lima: Ediciones Conejo, Colección 4, Suyus, s/f), Quijano critiques the way in which "modernity" was established in Latin America, but indicates the "bases for a different modernity" rooted in Latin American cultural traditions and in the historical and present experiences. See also the recent suggestive essay of Enrique Dussel, "Sistema mundo, dominacao e exclusao — Apontamentos sobre a historia do fenomeno religioso no proceso de globalizacao da America Latina," in *Historia da Igreja na America Latina e no Caribe, 1945-1995*, ed. Eduardo Hornaert (Petropolis/Sao Paulo: Vozes/CEHILA, 1995), pp. 39-79.

33. The expression "at least" may sound strange. It simply recognizes an important eschatological question which deserves more attention than it usually receives: Is the hope for the kingdom of God and for life eternal offered by the trinitarian God, the creator God, the God of dynamic love, compatible with the image of a static "heaven" and an "eternal" life without newness and growth, without creative dialogue? If we will become "as he [Jesus Christ] is," if God will be "all in all," it would be quasi-heretical to conceive of a hieratic eternity, "frozen" and uniform, which would finally amount to the same kind of "heaven" offered by some neoconservative expectations, where all growth is merely quantitative.

it possible to separate them without detracting from the very liberation we seek? As believers, is not the "freedom" Jesus Christ freely offers us the root and meaning of our participation in history?[34] Is it possible to renounce the "utopia of freedom" without destroying hope and removing the human quality of any search for liberation?

Personally, I propose a "strategy of patience": the effort to "untie the knots," trying to unravel the threads and preparing ourselves to reknit, on the loom of a different historical moment, a new social and theological understanding.

For that to occur, I believe it is essential to recover some of the threads of modernity's fabric. In other words, I believe the so-called liberal project represents the encounter and interaction of differing factors, partially divergent, which generate an unresolved tension throughout the length of modern history. In effect, it is not new to anyone that "modernity" has inherited a series of traditions in which, in different ways, are interwoven the "great biblical stories" and those of Mediterranean cultures, each of which, in turn, takes up and syncretizes a variety of elements. The multiple nature of this classic heritage is seen, for example, in the divergent ways in which classical antiquity is "recovered" on the one hand by the Italian and on the other by northern European renaissances. All this is melted and recast in the new scientific, technological, and economic mold that is forged in sixteenth-, seventeenth-, and eighteenth-century Europe, resulting in bourgeois industrial capitalism. The great statements of its ideology cover up the ambiguities of that history. The great themes of modernity — reason, liberty, the individual, democracy — are in fact understood and lived out in diverse, indeed, ambiguous and contradictory ways, in this lengthy historical process that develops from the end of the Middle Ages. Thus, *reason* is the human capacity to discern reality and to discern oneself freely and personally, without submitting to external authority, and it is also the technical rationality that resolves problems, at the service of the maximization of production and profit. *Liberty* is the inalienable right of each human being to dispose of oneself — the

34. This is the theme Elsa Tamez has developed magnificently in her interpretation of faith as liberation from all condemnation, universal in its purpose, that enables the appearance of a free human subject to serve all others in love. Elsa Tamez, *The Amnesty of Grace: Justification by Faith from a Latin American Perspective* (Nashville: Abingdon, 1993).

summary of the rights defined in secular terms by the French Revolution and in theistic terms by the American Revolution — and at the same time it is the "sacred" right to property which is solely protected in the free competitive market. The *individual* is the person-subject who takes up singularity and responsibility without getting lost in the collective, and is also the self-sufficient individual who defends privacy as a fortress, within which one is protected from all others. *Society,* therefore, may be understood as a "pact" which defends the countervailing interests of individuals (a la Hobbes) or as an inborn human structure that leads to the common welfare. *Democracy* is the "representative" government that assumes and replaces society and at the same time the "participatory" organization by which the community organizes its coexistence.

The "ands," "alsos," and "at the same times" of the previous paragraph could be multiplied. They are not balanced visions nor integrated elements of a synthesis. They are conflicting "motifs" that dispute the control of the ideological superstructure of societies, and also which coexist in conflict in an author or in authors close to each other, as can well be perceived in a careful comparison, for example, of G. Adam Smith's *The Theory of Moral Sentiments* (1759) and *The Wealth of Nations* (1776) or the previously noted divergence in the concept of liberalism between James Mill and his son John Stuart Mill. It is the growing tide of the triumph of (presumed) economic freedom, of technical reason, of competitive individualism, and of purely electoral democracy that leads to the shipwreck of humanist utopias from Kant to the utopian socialists — and even, we could say, to Marx!

Liberal Protestantism remained captive in this tragedy in two ways in Latin America: Its "liberal" discourse was used — in the slight measure of its social weight — to legitimate the most savage internal and external capitalism, while it was concurrently reinterpreted in sectors of its own constituency as an "ideology" of social improvement or as a "theology of prosperity." This is what we rightly perceived in the 1960s. Does this mean that today's Protestants should repudiate that heritage? My answer is: no! No, because it is the *Protestant inheritance of freedom, of self-identity, and of the responsibility of the person in the solidarity of community; of autonomy of human reason* (the reason of life and of active love) *in building the earthly city; of the rationality of hope in a history of which Jesus Christ is Lord.* What is involved is the reinterpretation of that history in search of a future, precisely as a response to the negation of all future implicit and explicit in the ideology and the politics of the "end of history." We claim the heritage of the utopian Protestantism to which Alves refers, but we claim it reinterpreted and re-lived in our time, with and from the marginalized of our societies, as a protest to the supposed "end of history" and as a program for the construction of a new historical project for our peoples.

2. The Evangelical Face of Latin American Protestantism

I. An Evangelical Protestantism

A. The Initiators of "Creole" Protestantism

THE INITIATORS WERE missionaries — largely North American or British (several Scots among these) — who arrived in Latin America from the 1840 decade onward. It is remarkable to note that, despite their confessional diversity (mostly Methodists, Presbyterians, and Baptists) and origin (North Americans and British), all shared the same theological horizon, which can be characterized as *evangelical* — using here the Anglo-Saxon connotation[1] — which Marsden, whose interpretation we are following in this section, defines very well:

1. It is not easy to find one's way in the jungle of meanings, hues, senses, connotations, denotations, and overlappings in the use of the word *evangélico* — what linguists would call a "polisemia." In English, dictionaries resolve its main meaning easily: *Evangelical* is defined as "relative to the gospels or the evangel." But problems arise in second or third meanings. The North American *Webster's New Collegiate Dictionary* speaks of a differentiation with "protestant" and engages in theological precisions, defining it as one branch of Protestantism which, originally within Anglicanism and later in the free churches, affirms "that the essence of the gospel consists principally in its doctrines of the sinful condition of man and his need for salvation, in the revelation of God's grace in Christ, in the need for a spiritual renewal and the participation in the experience of redemption through faith." Though more cautious, neither can the British *Oxford Students' Dictionary* evade the topic: "Those Protestants who underline the importance of

[Evangelicals] are people professing complete confidence in the Bible and preoccupied with the message of God's salvation of sinners through the death of Jesus Christ. Evangelicals were convinced that sincere acceptance of this "gospel" message was the key to virtue in this life and to eternal life in heaven; its rejection meant following the broad path that ended with the tortures of hell.[2]

We can all recognize in this summation the theology of pietism and of the Great Awakening of the eighteenth century which we associate with the names of Wesley and Whitefield in Great Britain and with Jonathan Edwards in the United States and which permeates most of Anglo-Saxon Protestantism — and surely the totality of its missionary ethos. This is the theological background of the mission to Latin America in its origins in the second half of the nineteenth century. However, this theology had undergone since midcentury significant influences worth noting. If we date — more or less arbitrarily — the year 1870 as a time for an evaluation, we would have to note the following data.

The *second awakening* (which we can associate with names such as Lyman Beecher, Timothy Dwight, and above all, Charles Finney), leading to Moody's great evangelistic and missionary crusade, had several particular characteristics:

1. It responded to the growth of urban populations, penetrated colleges and universities and middle-class commercial sectors, and had a religious prestige that rural or frontier "revivalism" had not attained.

2. Theologically it surpassed — as can be seen in Jonathan Edwards himself — the conflict between the Calvinist and the Arminian

---

personal faith and making amends for the death of Jesus Christ [?]." However, the term, as also the definition, is far from precise. Recent distinctions (especially in the United States) among "evangelicals," "conservative evangelicals," and "neo-evangelicals" do not clarify matters. In Germany, especially in Prussia, the term *evangelische* is adopted by various territorial churches with pietistic influences. To further confuse the picture, in Latin America the term *evangélico* is used undifferentiatedly for all churches that originated directly or indirectly from the Reformation, and in many cases it is virtually synonymous with *Protestant*. In this writing I have preferred to keep the equivocal nature of Latin American usage, hoping that the contexts will allow the reader to determine the meaning.

2. George M. Marsden, *Fundamentalism and American Culture: The Shaping of the Twentieth-Century Evangelicalism: 1870-1925* (New York and Oxford: Oxford University Press, 1980), p. 3.

traditions; in practice it admitted a certain free will (however it might be justified theologically) and the possibility of growth in holiness.

3. A high degree of subjectivism was added to the marked individualism of the first awakening. Someone has noted the difference between the hymnology of the first awakening, focused on the wonder of an ineffable grace (for example, Charles Wesley's "O, for a Thousand Tongues to Sing!" and even "Amazing Grace"), and the second awakening, which paused to describe the wonderful sentiments that grace awakens:

> Far away, in the depth of my spirit to-night
> Rings a melody sweeter than psalm;
> And in heavenly strains it unceasingly falls
> O'er my soul like an infinite calm.
>
> Peace, peace, wonderful peace,
> Coming down from the Father above;
> Sweep over my spirit for ever, I pray
> In fathomless billows of love.[3]

4. Religious awakening and social reformation (revival and reform) were seen as intimately related; the 1850 evangelists took upon themselves, along with the moral improvement of society, the cause of abolition of slavery and the struggle against poverty.

Once the Civil War ended (1865) the nation entered a period of optimism which was contagious as well to evangelicalism. The United States appears now as a model destined to inspire the whole world: the religious awakening, social progress, education — all mutually supported each other. In the words of a speaker in the New York 1873 Evangelical Alliance international meeting,

> Christianity is a universal philanthropist. It trains the youth; it feeds the hungry; it heals the sick. It rejoices in the increase of all the elements of material civilization. But it maintains that all those agencies are subordinate. The divine method of human improvement

---

3. "Far Away, in the Depth of My Spirit Tonight," of W. D. Connell, melody "Wonderful Peace." It was translated into Spanish by Vicente Mendoza and appears in Methodist and Baptist hymnals, and in those of various evangelical denominations at the beginning of the century throughout Latin America.

begins in human hearts through evangelical truth and it spreads from within outwardly till all is renewed.[4]

I do not believe proof is needed to affirm that this is the theology and piety which largely fed the vision of the first missionaries and which nourished the first converts. Many of the testimonies of the latter are quite stereotypical and follow a kind of "structure" that responds to the basic scheme of "evangelical soteriological theology." As a sample, compare a "summary" of the message with the witness of a woman convert — note both the polemic character and the "evangelical" content which both quotes bring together:

> *The evangelical Christian* believes: that Jesus came into the world to save sinners. That Jesus saves them if they wish to be saved. We are all sinners; He wants to save all. There is no other Savior. Jesus has all power. The church cannot save a soul, for it is necessary to be reborn.[5]

> "Christ, with his death, opened the doors of heaven to me. His shed blood washed away all my sins. Jesus paid what I, a sinner, owed to God's justice. By his mediation I attain forgiveness and not by means of a confessor. . . ."[6]

4. Joseph Angus, "Duty of the Church in Relation to Mission," in *History, Essays, Orations, and Other Documents of the Sixth General Conference of the Evangelical Alliance Held in New York, October 2-12, 1873,* ed. Philip Schaff and S. Irenaeus Prime (New York, 1874), p. 583.

5. Editorial, *El Estandarte Evangélico,* February 15, 1894, p. 2.

6. Ibid., December 20, 1894, p. 3. An interesting study on the reading of "testimonies" and their importance, which also indicates the necessity of a more intensive study of them, was presented at the meeting in Mexico on the occasion of the tenth anniversary of the death of Gonzalo Báez Camargo, by Carlos Garma Navarro: "Converts, Believers, and Cultural Change." It is evident that testimonies, "life stories," etc., constitute indispensable elements to recover the religious experience of Christian people (in our case, the Latin American Protestant people). At the same time, it is important to have in mind the particular characteristics of this type of material and the methodological care (basically the diverse forms of what sociologists call "triangulation") which should be taken in evaluating this material. See, among others, the methodological observations in Thomas Robbins, *Cults, Converts, and Charisma: The Sociology of New Religious Movements* (London: SAGE Publications, 1988), and the very interesting article of R. Stephen Warner, "Oenology: The Making of New Wine," a field study in a Presbyterian church in California, in Anthony Orum, Joe Fagin, and Gideon Sjoberg, *A Case for the Case Study* (Berkeley: University of California Press, 1991), pp. 175-95. In *Baptist*

Undoubtedly, both in the message of the missionaries and in the consciousness of the new congregations, there were differences due to the peculiar situation of this "mission field." One was the priority of the anti-Catholic polemic, which took up major space in Protestant publications of the time, at once repeating the classic arguments of the seventeenth- and eighteenth-century controversies and denouncing cases of corruption, obscurantism, or authoritarianism of the Roman Catholic Church or its representatives. For that reason it was necessary to furnish new converts with knowledge and arguments for this conflict. That need led to a great emphasis on study of the Bible and of the basic doctrines of Protestantism. Another peculiarity was the special importance and use given to the Bible, which was exalted both as a "weapon" in the "struggle against error" and as an indispensable tool for evangelization. In both senses, Scripture was conceived as having a "power," a certain intrinsic efficacy that reproves, convinces, and converts. Finally, the need to secure social space for personal and community life and development obliged the believer to be concerned with political conditions that assured that possibility: religious liberty; secularization of services such as education, marriage, and cemeteries; nondiscrimination in work and education, including concern for the condition of the poor. However, one must note that this "public dimension" did not become directly integrated in their faith's horizon; it remained as a derived "consequence" or as an "independent" sphere in which one must witness honestly and responsibly. When social conditions no longer seemed to require a defense of freedoms, these positions were easily left behind.

B. Changes in the Evangelical Theological Horizon

It is the key ideas and attitudes of this evangelical theology which model the faith and life of the congregations that were formed throughout these decades and which dominated Creole Protestantism at least until the Great War. Little by little, nevertheless, differences began to appear — still larvate in 1916 — whose effects have marked Latin American Protestantism to this day. To understand them we have to return to the North American scene. There, "evangelical" Protestantism confronted,

---

Battles (New Brunswick and London: Rutgers University Press), 1990, Nancy Ammerman offers an interesting methodological excursus in Appendices A and B, pp. 287-340.

during the last third of the century, the challenges of an urban culture reclaimed by secularism, a science that questioned Christian "truths" which were considered fundamental, and theological liberalism — generically called "modernism" — which seemed to endanger the trustworthiness of Scripture and of central elements of evangelical Christology and soteriology. How did "evangelical" Protestantism react to these challenges? Let us briefly review three aspects: evangelical "piety," social ethics, and the "defense of the faith."

1. What characterized evangelical piety in the last decades of the nineteenth century was "the holiness movement," what Marsden termed "the victorious life." Here were united, as indicated earlier, the Wesleyan sanctification and perfection tradition with the Calvinist permanent struggle against sin. Both coincided in affirming a "baptism of the Holy Spirit" which allowed the believer to be liberated from the power of sin and to live a "victorious" Christian life. "To be full of the Spirit," to be "wholly consecrated," and similar phrases constituted the symbolic language of this piety, such as was expressed, for example, in the well-known hymn of Havergal:

Take my life and let it be
Consecrated, Lord, to Thee;
Take my moments and my days,
Let them flow in ceaseless praise.

Take my hands and let them move
At the impulse of Thy love;
Take my feet and let them be
Swift and beautiful for Thee.

(Other lines relate "my voice," "lips," "silver and gold," "intellect," "will," "heart," "love," "myself"!)[7]

In the world of the Wesleyan tradition, the insistence on the experience of the "second blessing" — the fullness of sanctification — gave rise to divisions in the face of what some considered to be an

---

7. It is interesting to note that Francis R. Havergal (1836-79) had a conversion experience in 1850 that he describes as follows: "I committed my soul to the Saviour and earth and heaven were brighter from that moment." Havergal was Anglican, of a "mildly Calvinist" theology, says a biographer, and of "evangelical" experience ("I believe," he said, "in free and full salvation"). One could hardly better illustrate the synthesis that dominated this movement.

abandonment of the search for holiness by Methodist churches; thus were born — in addition to the Salvation Army (England, 1880) — the Church of God (Anderson, Indiana, 1880), the Christian and Missionary Alliance (1887), the Church of the Nazarene (1908), and the Pilgrim Holiness Church (1897). The importance of this development for our topic becomes clear when one sees how soon after their formation (between 1897 and 1914) all these churches entered Latin America. In the Reformed evangelical tradition, the holiness movement had the same vigor and emphasis. It moved, however, toward a greater doctrinal concern, as seen in its participation in the creation of the Keswick Conferences group and the "Prophecy Conferences" that became immediate antecedents of fundamentalism.

2. David Moberg spoke of "the great reversal" produced in North American evangelicalism in the first decades of the twentieth century with regard to social concern.[8] In effect, from the "revival and reform" formula it moved to the alternative "evangelization or social reform." This change seemed to occur in two stages: a first one, from 1870 to 1900, meant a withdrawal from the political sphere and a concentration on the private sphere as a means of social reform, focusing action in the sphere of charity; and a second one in which, as Marsden said, "all progressive social concern, whether political or private, became suspect among revivalist evangelicals and was relegated to a very minor role."[9] Historians tend to suggest three causes. (a) The Methodist holiness model triumphed over the Reformed tradition, which had been closely tied in the United States to the "building of the kingdom of God" in America. Hence, holiness was disconnected from history to become an individual subjective experience — or at most belonging to the small "community" — that reduced service to charitable action. (b) The charismatic experience of living in a kind of "new dispensation," an "era of the Holy Spirit" which is disconnected from "salvation history," relegates the Old Testament and consequently erodes the basis for the Reformed concern for a divine law that should also be instituted in society. The growing predominance of premillennialism and subsequently of the dispensationalism introduced by John Nelson Darby and

8. *The Great Reversal: Evangelism versus Social Concern* (Philadelphia: Lippincott, 1972). Cf. Donald Dayton, *Discovering an Evangelical Heritage* (New York, 1976), and Richard Pierard, *The Unequal Yoke* (Philadelphia, 1970).

9. Marsden, p. 86.

widely extended in the evangelical world, consecrated this separation by declaring the "dispensations" (time periods) of "human government" and "law" already passed and terminated, stages in a process which lack all direct relevance for the present "dispensation," the time of grace, whose only meaning and object is the preaching of the gospel of personal salvation. (c) The appearance, since 1910, of the Social Gospel, perceived as a form of modernism or theological liberalism and a denial of fundamental doctrines of the faith, evoked a rejection in evangelical circles. C. I. Scofield, one of the most successful champions of dispensationalism and a significant presence in Latin America, stated unequivocally that Christ's only reply to slavery, intemperance, prostitution, unequal distribution of wealth, and the oppression of the weak was to preach regeneration through the Holy Spirit.[10]

3. What we call *fundamentalism* is a complex phenomenon; it would be ridiculous to try to tackle it in a few lines. Nevertheless, it is essential to give it some attention, with one warning: We refer only to fundamentalism as a phenomenon of the evangelical world at the end of the nineteenth century and beginning of the twentieth.[11] The first historical observation of importance is that it is useful to distinguish a

---

10. Marsden's summary, n. 30, p. 255, in *C. I. Scofield's Question Box*, comp. Ella A. Poble (Chicago: Moody Bible Institute, n.d.), *Record of Christian Work* n/d.

11. The subject of "fundamentalism" has regained actuality as a religious or religio-political phenomenon which arises in various religions (for example, in Judaism and Islam) as well as in political movements characterized by authoritarianism or intransigence. In this regard, of interest is the research directed and edited by Martin Marty and R. Scott Appleby, *Fundamentalisms Observed* (Chicago: University of Chicago Press, 1991), and the evaluation by the same editors in their work, *The Glory and Power: The Fundamentalist Challenge to the Modern World* (Boston: Beacon Press, 1992). Some thirty years ago an unusual North American writer, Eric Hoffer, tried to find in character traits, social experiences of "frustration" and a particular "mentality," common characteristics to various mass movements — religious, social, or political — that he defines as forms of fanaticism: the personality he called "the true believer." Though he does not refer specifically to fundamentalism, evidently it is an attempt to find the "psychological structures" that correspond to what we today call by that name; Eric Hoffer, *The True Believer* (New York: Harper and Row, 1966). Subsequently there have been many efforts in the same direction. The work of Marty and Appleby, *The Glory and Power*, includes observations in this regard. Nevertheless, though among all these movements there exist a series of analogous psychological elements and political attitudes, I do not think it best to deal with this topic in such general terms. They are movements that arise within defined historical contexts and which must be considered first of all in the light of those contexts and not as mere "cases" of a generalized phenomenon.

first stage that extends more or less to the beginning of the Great War, and a second stage, far more spectacular, following that war. Following Marsden, we characterize these stages, respectively, as "a defense of the faith" and "the defense of Christian America."

a. Fundamentalism appeared as the *reaction of a faith which felt itself threatened by the advance of secularism and by a science that denied the reality of the supernatural.* How to respond? Basically there were two responses that reflected two philosophic views. One distinguishes the level of science from that of religion: The first is the sphere of objective facts; the second is that of subjective experience, of feeling — we could say it is the expression of the romantic heritage of American culture. Others, however, knew only one criterion of truth, that of the concrete facts and data of reality which anyone can observe; it is the tradition of "common sense" of Scottish origin that predominated in North American thought.[12]

For the latter perspective it was essential to have an infallible source, specific and irrefutable, to affirm the realities of the supernatural world with the same force as "common sense" affirms those of the natural world. They found that in the Scriptures. Hence, when scientific discoveries seemed to enter into conflict with the affirmations of Scripture, what was involved was either an erroneous scientific hypothesis or an erroneous interpretation of Scripture. The various forms of "harmonization" started from this premise. In addition, the only criterion that could be applied to the reading of the Bible was that the texts must be read and interpreted "literally" (unless they themselves indicated otherwise). Of course, "literally" meant in this instance a positivistic interpretation as objective data provable by observation and reason (so in a quite different sense from what the term had in medieval usage or in that of Luther). Plenary and verbal inspiration, literal and inerrant interpretation were the indispensable walls to protect the truth of faith. That was fundamentalism.

Such a posture would seem to demand total *intransigence:* there are no gray zones between truth and error. Not all in the revivalist and holiness movement were disposed toward such intransigence. Moody, for example, advised: "Let us hold to truth, but by all means let us hold

---

12. On the importance of the Scottish philosophic school of common sense realism in the rise of fundamentalism in North America, see Marty and Appleby, *The Glory and Power,* pp. 59-60, and Marsden, *Fundamentalism and American Culture,* pp. 14-16, 110-16.

to it in love, and not with a theological club." In the Reformed tradition, nonetheless, such concession rang of indifference: "We are constantly told in our day that we ought not to attack error but simply to teach the truth. This is the method of the coward and the trimmer; it was not the method of Christ," responded Torrey, one of Moody's associates.[13] Both positions have always existed within fundamentalism, but it is evident that the latter had the greater ascendance and to this day defines the profile of fundamentalism.

In the combination of literalism and intransigence there entered the theme of *premillennialism*. As such, the premillennial interpretation had always existed in eschatological discussions. That is, we live prior to the millennium, which will inaugurate a new time that will precede the establishment of the kingdom of God (with diverse views regarding the succession and nature of the forthcoming events). The dominant view in Protestantism in general, and in North American Protestantism in particular, had been largely postmillennial; that is, the apocalyptic promises of the millennium, the outpouring of the Spirit, the struggle against the Antichrist (frequently identified as the pope or heads of other religions) would happen in this time and would lead to a golden age, the millennium of Revelation 20, the final epoch of current history, where the outpouring of the Spirit would occur and the gospel would spread throughout the world, and at the end of which Christ would return and history would come to its end. In the optimistic and secularistic mood of the second half of the nineteenth century, the postmillennial vision becomes more "naturalized": The way of the kingdom came to be identified with human progress and the advances of North American culture, which were seen as signs of a future in which the unity of religion and of civilization's progress would create a new era of peace, justice, and prosperity.

This "natural" eschatology, of which the Social Gospel was — and still is — accused, could only be repugnant for an evangelical faith. On the one hand, it was seen as a denial of transcendence (in the terminology of that day, the "supernatural"). On the other hand, it transformed the biblical revelation into a "poetic fantasy" about a history which human beings shape and control — and such a thing was totally incompatible with the concept of the truth of "common sense realism." Premillennial-

---

13. "What Was Christ's Attitude toward Error: A Symposium," *Record of Christian Work*, November 1899, pp. 600, 602; cited in Stanley N. Gundry, *Love Them In: The Proclamation Theology of D. L. Moody* (Chicago, 1976), pp. 217-18.

ism appears, therefore, as a countercultural reaction which denies to secular culture all eschatological pretension; this history, this society, and these churches, insofar as some of them adapt to the world, are a field of combat where the true gospel must be preached and men and women called to unite in the eschatological congregation that awaits the "rapture," the beginning of the millennium, or "the Lord's appearance."

The Scot John Nelson Darby gave this vision a biblical hermeneutic based on interpretation of the books of Daniel and Revelation, called dispensationalism, which had enormous influence on the evangelical world. His North American disciple, C. I. Scofield, published a translation of the Bible, the notes of which systematically applied this interpretation to all of Scripture, that was widely circulated. While in Great Britain, Darby gave rise to an independent denomination — the Plymouth Brethren and the Free Brethren, and the churches that resulted from these — in the United States the movement lived within the existing churches.[14]

The "defense of faith" became concrete in *the defense of the Scriptures* with the characteristics we have indicated above. In a sense, however, the Bible is not just a "means" for the defense of the faith but an "object of faith" that acquires a certain autonomy. In his book *Fundamentalism,* the Englishman James Barr expresses it thus:

> For fundamentalists the Bible is more than the source of verity for their religion, more than the essential source or textbook. It is part of the religion itself, indeed it is practically the center of religion. . . . In the fundamentalist mind the Bible functions as a sort of correlative of Christ, a verbalized, "inscripturated" entity, the given form of words in which God has made himself known. . . . While Christ is the divine Lord and Savior, the Bible is the supreme religious symbol that is tangible, articulate, possessable, accessible to men on earth.[15]

Of course, Christ is ontologically above Scripture, but epistemologically Christ is subordinated to Scripture. Therefore it is essential to have the Bible, to revere it, to grant it a place of honor in mind and heart, but

---

14. There is an interesting intepretation of the pre- and postmillenarian eschatology summarized by Marty and Appleby, *The Glory and Power,* pp. 48-52. Also a good theological discussion of the subject in James Barr, *Fundamentalism* (London: SCM Press, 1977), passim.

15. Barr, p. 36.

also at the dining room table or night table by the bed. Some way or other, it is the icon and sacrament of faith.

b. Perhaps it is not so strange that this countercultural movement became, especially during and after the Great War, the support of a culture: *the defense of Christian America*. In the end, every widely accepted symbolic universe plays a cultural role in society. It is not for us now to investigate the birth of this phenomenon, but neither can we fail to note it, because it plays a significant role in the missionary movement. Within evangelical fundamentalism, several distinct attitudes toward culture and society coexisted. What we might call mediating attitudes, however, pre-dominated, represented by a reaffirmation of what was considered the "American evangelical tradition" ("the old-time religion") that should be defended against the advances of secularism, modernism, and immorality. The tradition was represented, for example, by the sadly famous William J. Bryan of the "monkey trial," which became known worldwide in the theatrical version of *Inherit the Wind*. There was also a more Reformed strand which promoted a transformation of culture on the basis of Christian teaching: for example, within fundamentalism, that of Professor J. Gresham Machen at Princeton.

The Great War (1914-18) radicalized positions. Almost until the United States entered the conflict, fundamentalist evangelical groups were reticent with regard to the war — the world was headed toward its end, wars could not improve anything. From 1917 on, however, there was a change. The millennial interpretations were revised and to the two who classically represented the Antichrist (the pope and the Muslims), Bismarck was added. To participate in the war was a Christian duty:

> The Kaiser boldly threw down the gage of battle: infidel Germany [the crib of theological liberalism] against the believing world — Kultur against Christianity — the gospel of Hate against the Gospel of Love. Thus is Satan personified — "Myself and God." . . . Never did Crusader lift battle-axe in a holier war against the Saracen than is waged by our soldiers of the cross against the German.[16]

Three elements fill out the picture of fundamentalism at the close of the war: the addition of "Communist Bolshevism" to the Antichrist trinity

---

16. Cited in Marsden, *Fundamentalism and American Culture*, p. 151; a quote of Henry Watterson in *The King's Business* 9 (December 1918): 1026-27, editorial of *Louisville Courier Journal*.

— now replacing the defeated Kaiser; the battle to eradicate from North American culture all that might threaten pure evangelical faith — hence the Scopes judgment against teaching evolution in schools[17] and other similar crusades, and the transfer of struggle to the rural South which thus legitimated religiously its conflict with the industrial North.

We are, to be sure, referring to general features: Things are always more nuanced and diversified than these brief paragraphs suggest. Nonetheless, this presentation seems to me a basically correct way to understand aspects of our Latin American Protestantism.[18] How did all this affect the churches? Historians tend to speak of three variants. (i) Among the more traditional denominations — Episcopalians, Presbyterians, Methodists, Baptists — internal groupings carried the battle into the heart of the denominations, with more success in some than in others, but without being able to systematically "expel" their adversaries or to take national control of the denomination. (Without doubt the hardest battles took place in the Southern Baptist Convention[19] and in the two major Presbyterian churches.) (ii) In some denominations, especially in the holiness churches and in the nascent Pentecostal movements, their pietistic and evangelical tradition was remolded by fundamentalist influence. (iii) Some of the more extreme fundamentalists, particularly the dispensationalists for whom "separation" was an article of faith, formed their own denominations.[20]

---

17. On the subject of creation and evolution, which strangely has reappeared in discussions on education in electoral campaigns in several U.S. states as recently as the end of 1994, see Marty and Appleby, *The Glory and Power*, pp. 53-56. Somewhat unexpectedly, a strong religious opposition (mostly from the Catholic sector) appeared in Argentina in the discussion of "basic contents" for high school education, rejecting even a mention of Darwin. The secretary of education found it necessary to heed these protests, precipitating a crisis in which several well-known educators who had worked in the preparation of the "contents" resigned their posts.

18. The fundamentalist phenomenon, particularly in the Anglo-Saxon world, has been interpreted in diverse ways: as a countercultural reaction, as a form of "nativism," as a manifestation of premillenarianism, and also (by the German author Riesenbrandt) as "radical patriarchalism."

19. With regard to the conflicts in the Southern Baptist Convention, there is a fascinating, careful, and balanced study by Nancy Ammerman, *Baptist Battles*, to which we referred in note 6.

20. G. W. Dollar, *A History of Fundamentalism in America* (Greenville, S.C.: Bob Jones University Press, 1973), Intro., 7; V:14; XXI:32. The book is of interest as a history of fundamentalism as seen from within fundamentalism.

II. Growth and Diversification

A. "Atomization of Protestantisms"

Thus did Jean-Pierre Bastian entitle the period between 1949 and 1959. I feel this description is inadequate, for it presupposes a prior Protestant identity defined by the "liberal option." The error stems, I believe, from judging identity on the basis of the views of missionary and local leaders represented in conferences, and not giving sufficient attention to the development of evangelical piety as the real substratum of Latin American missionary Protestantism. The interpretation of Hans-Jürgen Prien is no better, for it tends to lump together the majority of North American missions as pietistic, conservative, and fundamentalist, without clarifying what is specifically meant by those terms. Only Pablo Deiros is more nuanced and careful in analyzing the period he calls "Development," which is located between 1930 and 1960.[21] He agrees with the others in distinguishing three main trends in Latin American Protestantism, which he characterizes as liberationists, conservatives, and fundamentalists.[22] In his presentation, however,[23] it becomes evident that what is involved are "tendencies" that are present in the "evangelical world" as a whole, although they appear as more pronounced in one or another church. This is not the definition of a typology that permits a distinction between the churches.

I think that, in order to properly understand this topic, it is necessary to start with the previous period. *My thesis is that toward 1916 Latin American missionary Protestantism was basically "evangelical" according to the model of the American evangelicalism of the "second awakening": individualistic, Christological-soteriological in a basically subjective key, with emphasis on sanctification. It had a genuine social interest, expressed in charity and mutual aid, but did not have a structural and political perspective save as it touched upon the defense of its own liberty and the struggle against all discriminations. Therefore, it tended politically to be liberal and democratic, but without sustaining that option in its faith nor making it an integral part of its piety.*

21. Pablo A. Deiros, *Historia del Cristianismo en América Latina* (Buenos Aires: Latin America Theological Fraternity, 1992). See, by the same author, "Protestant Fundamentalism in Latin America," in Marty and Appleby, *Fundamentalisms Observed,* 1:142-96.

22. Deiros, *Historia del Cristianismo en América Latina,* p. 802.

23. Ibid., pp. 803-6.

From the postwar period on (1918 and following) changes begin to take place within this fundamental pattern. The analysis of these modifications is crucial in order to understand the phenomenon Bastian describes as "atomization." Such analysis, however, will only be possible to the extent that we engage in a historical research that seriously deals with the history of mentalities, life stories, investigation into daily life — in a word, that recovers the objective and subjective "life" of evangelical communities and not just their formal and institutional aspects. Meanwhile, I dare to suggest some clues and hypotheses:

1. From the beginning of this century, but even more so after the Great War and rapidly since 1930, evangelical Protestantism grew with a series of missions that represented the holiness movement and millennial and fundamentalist streams from Great Britain and the United States. Moreover, after the Second World War a new wave of missionaries arrived when China, India, and other Eastern countries become closed to Western missions. Prudencio Damboriena, always obsessed with this "missionary invasion," speaks of 1,707 foreign missionaries in 1916 and 6,361 in 1957.[24] One must also note that the "classical" "mother" churches (Methodist, Presbyterian, Baptist) were strongly influenced by these movements. *All evangelical Protestantism absorbed in great measure the characteristics of this evangelical "new wave": a more marked dualism and spirituality, an ethic of withdrawal from the world accompanied by legalistic rigidity.*[25]

2. On the crest of a wave of social mobility, class "mentality" defined itself in evangelical Protestantism in the direction of the emerging middle sectors. In this context we should locate, in my judgment, the more profound relationship between Protestantism and bourgeois liberalism. What evangelical Protestantism (and perhaps also "immigra-

24. Prudencio Damboriena, S.J., *El Protestantismo en América Latina* (Friburgo: FERES, 1962), 1:32. Damboriena explains this growth mainly in terms of the relocation of missions, missionaries, and resources displaced by the loss of mission fields in Asia (China, Indochina, etc.), pp. 27-45. Other statistics he gives for the same period suggest that an outside cause is not a sufficient explanation; for example, the increase of local workers from 2,176 to 14,299 or that of full members from 170,827 to 4,230,413.

25. For instance, it is interesting to note that in 1894 in *El Estandarte Evangélico* it was possible to discuss freely the use of wine in Methodist homes, without one side or the other making it an article of faith. But toward 1930 the vote of abstinence and the white ribbon that indicated it were almost a requirement for membership in the Latin American Methodist church.

tion" Protestantism) contributes to the development of Latin American bourgeois liberalism is not so much the political or commercial U.S. influence, nor even the shift of an ideology as such, but *a series of attitudes and a horizon of meaning generated by the very experience of conversion which coincides with the upward mobility aspirations of certain sectors of society and with the "ethos" of bourgeois liberalism.*

The sociological categories of Max Weber or the structural analysis of Durkheim are here more useful to understand this phenomenon than political theory or economic determinisms. Elsewhere I have tried to point out some data for this type of analysis, which I shall not now repeat. It has to do, in synthesis, with indicating how the call to conversion as a personal, total, and transforming decision, which is at the very center of evangelization, means the re-creation of an identity, the construction of a subject who feels able to decide for himself/herself, responsibly and freely — "you have to decide," "you are alone before the Savior" — with a new self-consciousness that encourages the taking of initiatives.[26] With regard to Pentecostalism, Douglas Peterson has spoken in this regard of an "assertiveness," a certain "attitude of initiative" as a concomitant of the conversion experience and of the new roles that people assume in community. If to this we add a series of ethical values, we have the picture of persons eminently prepared for the liberal-modernizing model.

3. Insofar as this class mentality took root and, in successive decades, more and more evangelicals indeed entered the modest middle classes, the political and social stream of socialism and communism became as unacceptable as the "antireligious" stance. Though I cannot prove it, I dare to think that until the 1920s, the majority of evangelicals in the lower and middle classes leaned toward democratic parties that assured religious freedom — the center-left Radical parties in Argentina or Chile, Colorados in Uruguay, liberals in Colombia, the PRI in Mexico — but from those years on they reacted ever more strongly against the ideology of "the left." Admiration for "American democracy," the anti-communism of U.S. fundamentalism after the 1920s, and their class ideology carried them in this direction. They did not yet turn to the right, given its clerical connection, but they would not take too long to feel attracted by the military rhetoric of morals, order, and stability.

26. Cf. "Historia y Misión," in *Protestantismo y Liberalismo* (San José, Costa Rica: DEI, 1983), pp. 15-36.

4. The tension that always existed in the alliance of Protestantism and liberalism as "partners" in the struggle for democratization and against the conservative and clerical sectors became more polemical when the more moderate intellectuals were followed, toward the end of the nineteenth century, by the harsh antireligious militancy of free thought and of Positivism.[27] In the River Plate, for example, stemming especially from Spanish anarchism, there appeared translations of Feuerbach, Baur, and Strauss and works of Renan and other "modernist" authors, which circulated in union libraries and among supporters of socialism and anarchism and were taken up by some intellectuals. In 1906 Clemente Ricci published in the evangelical journal *La Reforma* (and republished as a book in 1922) a translation of the Italian professor Aníbal Fiori's refutation of the famous book of Milesbo (Emilio Mossi), "Jesus Christ Never Existed." This attack on Christian faith had been translated into Spanish in 1906. Writing in 1928, Ricardo Rojas shows in his *The Invisible Christ* considerable knowledge of some aspects of higher criticism, of the works of Renan, Binet Sanglé, and others. One need not think this exceptional. Examples could be multiplied, at both "cultured" and "popular" levels. The "struggle for the faith" was present also on this front.

5. This is the situation into which fundamentalism — and perhaps particularly premillenarian fundamentalism — was received. Though Darbyists (Free Brethren) and other fundamentalist and premillenarian denominations (Adventists, Christian Alliance, Evangelical Union) were in Latin America from the century's beginning, the debates on these topics did not seem to get going until considerably later. In a manual of *Great Biblical Truths* published by the Free Brethren as late as 1944,[28] these themes do not appear among the fundamental doctrines and appear only indirectly in the discussion of various subjects. On the other hand, already in the Evangelical Conference of Montevideo in 1925, tension is evident in two themes. One concerned the "theological status" attributed to

27. On this transition, see Leopoldo Zea, *The Latin American Mind* (Norman: University of Oklahoma Press, 1963). Concerning the ideological significance of this transition, Zea makes in another writing an interesting comment which, *mutatis mutandis*, perhaps applies also to evangelicals: "the discussion about freedom is abandoned and the order is established which will allow material progress in each country and, with it, freedom as an extra added." *Las ideas en Iberoamérica en el siglo XIX* (La Plata: Universidad Nacional de La Plata, Departamento de Filosofía, 1956), p. 43.

28. Originally articles in *El Sendero del Creyente*, vol. 35; compiled in the book by the same title, 1945.

Catholicism. For some it was a church with which we differ on some matters, for others it was a church that had deviated from the gospel, for others still it was a form of masked paganism or the Antichrist. The other subject, less explicit, was the attitude toward theological liberalism — debated at times as the conflict of priority options for evangelization or for social action, or as critique of the Social Gospel, or even in the very definition of "gospel." When the "gospel" was defined in the Montevideo Report, it began with Harnack's trilogy, "the fatherhood of God," it continued in classical Protestant terms with the "centrality of Christ," and it was completed "evangelically" with "sin and the need for repentance."[29]

6. The sharpness of the conflict took diverse expressions in different countries. Yet toward the end of the 1940s it was very strong, and it is not arbitrary that Bastian should have located it in 1949 at the Latin American Protestant Conference (CELA I) in Buenos Aires. There was a wide representativity there, but symbolically there burst into the conference representatives of the International Evangelical Council of Carl McIntyre. Unanimously the conference rejected this "putsch" tactic to enter the proceedings, but there is no doubt that their denunciation of liberal and communist modernism had its impact. Churches and sectors of churches in Brazil were soon affected by the movement, and everywhere — even if without organic commitment — separatist fundamentalism grew in various denominations. Subsequent history does not need much greater detail. A good summary is presented in Deiros's *History of Christianity in Latin America*.[30] Existing Protestant organizations with wide participation — councils, youth federations, united evangelization campaigns — either broke up or had to take sides in this confrontation. The sectors interested in maintaining an active social witness joined together (often with international "ecumenism") and created their own organizations (Movimiento Estudiantil Crisitiano [MEC], Iglesia y Sociedad en América Latina [ISAL], Misión Urbana e Industrial [MISUR], and Consejo Ecuménico de Educación Cristiana [CELADEC]). In various ways they sought a theological articulation in dialectic theology or in a "theology of God's work in history." However, most evangelical churches did not participate in their movements, nor were they accepted or supported by a sizable part of church memberships (nor at times of the leadership) in the very churches from which they came. Around 1960 one could note

---

29. *Christian Work in Latinamerica* (Montevideo: CCLA, 1926), 1:350.
30. Deiros, *Historia del Cristianismo en América Latina*, pp. 771f., 801-8.

very clearly this crisis in the discussions of CELA (Conferencia Evangélica Latinoamericana) II, 1961, and even more so in CELA III, 1965. The fragmentation was later even more evident, ecumenicals or evangelicals, CLAI (Consejo Latinoamericano de Iglesias) or CONELA (Confraternidad Evangélica Latinoamericana), "right" or "left," "evangelicals" or "liberationists." No "third alternatives" were accepted.

7. A new factor strengthened the opposition. Changes since the 1950s and more particularly since Vatican Council II, which seemed to bring Catholicism closer to Protestant positions, led evangelical churches and leaders to adopt an attitude of dialogue — without doubt stimulated by the ecumenical movement. The transition from the harsh condemnation of the Roman Catholic Church as "antievangelical" to its recognition as even a possible "partner" in the evangelizing mission was more than the more conservative evangelical sectors could tolerate. It was seen as simply "treason to the gospel."

What seems important to note — and this is my thesis at this point — is that *it was not a matter of churches versus churches, or denominations versus denominations.* Though some churches in some countries leaned in one direction or the other and some were clearly aligned with the "evangelical" sector, *the crisis cut through all denominations and even local congregations.* The rupture, internal and external, seemed absolute and definitive. Toward 1990, Bastian's thesis of "atomization" seems justified.

III. Shadows and Lights in "the Evangelical"

The "atomization" and "identity crisis" of Latin American Protestantism, of which so much is said, are closely linked to the development of this process in the "evangelical world" and to the answers and reactions awakened within the Protestant camp as a whole. Relating the evangelical movement we have just outlined to Pentecostalism, Bastian speaks of "a sectarian and millennialist Protestantism" which, between the 1930s and 1949, "burst outside and independently from established Protestantism of liberal origin." Setting aside for the moment the identification of Pentecostalism with the Protestant evangelical process of the preceding decades, it seems to me erroneous to speak about "outside and independently." The kinship of origin, of piety, and even of theology and the interpenetration of earlier and later missionary waves force us to consider the phenomenon as "internal to evangelical missionary Protestantism" in

Latin America. What I have termed "the evangelical face of Latin American Protestantism" defines its identity from the outset up to the present. *The identity of Latin American Protestantism is unthinkable if these features are excluded. Even more, I would dare to say that the future of Latin American Protestantism will be evangelical or it will not be.* Precisely for that reason, it is important to become aware of negative processes and directions that have taken place in our Protestant history.

A. *The influence of extreme fundamentalism, divisive and largely, if not exclusively, premillennial, has had negative effects on evangelical Protestantism in the following ways:*

1. It has tied us to, and has been the transmission belt of, the worst features of United States ideology and politics — to the point of leading churches and church leaders to assume as their own the reactionary ideological campaigns of the "new religious right" of the United States, and to support the "security regimes" and the repressive policies which during the last decades accompanied those regimes. (The examples of Chile, Guatemala, and the material and ideological backing of the "contras" in Nicaragua suffice to illustrate our point.)[31]

2. In the field of ethics, it has developed the most vulnerable aspects of the evangelical and pietistic tradition: legalism and self-justification, the opposition between the material and the spiritual, and the "withdrawal from the world" which in practice leads to a dual morality and to introverted social and political criteria. It is enough that a government allow or favor the churches for it to be acceptable; "we have the freedom to preach" is often the reply when the brutal violation of human rights by such governments is pointed out.

3. In ecclesiastical life, the "doctrine of separation" has led to isolation and division.

4. The worst, however, seems to me to be the doctrinal distortion which at once legitimates and reinforces these tendencies. I dare to say that this type of fundamentalism has produced, in several ways, a caricature of the authentic evangelical profile.[32]

31. The development of this line in North American fundamentalist sectors has been widely studied. The best reference I know is the study by Erling Jorstad, *The New Christian Right: 1981-1988* (Lewiston/Queenston: Edwin Mellen Press, 1987), with excellent bibliographical notes.

32. A recent work by George M. Marsden, *Understanding Fundamentalism and Evangelicalism* (Grand Rapids: Eerdmans, 1991), is very illuminating for understanding the relationship between "evangelicalism" and recent developments in fundamentalism.

a. The rich and transforming faith experience becomes the acceptance of a narrow and stereotypical theological scheme, badly named "the plan of salvation," as if it were a computer where certain keys should be pressed to obtain the desired results.

b. The recognition of the centrality of the biblical Word illumined by the power of the Holy Spirit becomes a "bibliolatry" subject to an arbitrary and rationalistic hermeneutic; instead of the rich treasure from which the wise scribe "brings out what is new and what is old" (Matt. 13:52), the study of the Bible becomes an exercise of permanent repetition.

c. In place of the richness of the fraternal communion in Jesus Christ of the Lutheran *collegia pietatis,* of the Methodist "classes" and "groups," or of the Baptist congregations, premillennialism empties the community of faith of all theological meaning, transforming the church into a kind of "waiting room" for the millennium, without any soteriological significance.

d. This same scheme transforms human history into a series of numbers and signs to be deciphered instead of a space where the power of Jesus Christ opens the way and invites us to share in his struggle. Thus, the joyful expectation of the *"parousia* of the Lord" becomes a guessing game of additions and subtractions of years and dates.

Indeed, I have participated in enough services and meetings, and have had a brotherly relationship with too many men and women of this persuasion, not to know that this is a caricature when it refers to their concrete Christian life: I have seen there the joy of salvation, transformed lives, brotherly love, solidarity and service, witness in the world, and even sharing in the causes of justice and peace. Jesus Christ is larger than our images of him, and the Spirit is more powerful than our paltry expectations and works *in spite of* our theological distortions. Nevertheless, I have also seen the evil these distortions have caused: the sterile debates, unnecessary divisions, lost opportunities for witness, and the counter-witness in the private and public lives of churches and believers. No church has a monopoly on these negative elements, and no church is exempt from them, but it is good to identify them within and beyond our house to be able to correct them.

B. Naturally, a question arises: *If it has so many negative aspects, how is it possible that this tendency should have had, and has, such a wide presence in our churches?*

1. Undoubtedly there are social factors — which we have already indicated — that contributed to it. On the other hand, Rubem Alves has analyzed very acutely the psychological aspects linked to the quest for security and to the sense of power that operate in this fundamentalism — which he analyzes profoundly as the "correct doctrine Protestantism" of his own church of origin. Nor can we silence the realities of pride, indiscriminate accusations, and mocking self-sufficiency with which we — liberal Protestants — have responded to fundamentalism and thereby only confirmed it.

2. There is, however, a positive element which I consider more important. Faced with the positivistic and atheistic streams coming from society and with some theological currents from within Protestantism which seemed to empty the content of evangelical faith, *many evangelicals saw fundamentalism as the only barrier they could raise up against their enemies, the only defense of a faith that gave meaning to life.* If at the hands of atheistic critique and theological liberalism they were at risk of losing the Scriptures from whose pages they had received the message of salvation; if the fervor of their piety would become cool in a religion as formal and ritualistic as what they had left behind at their conversion; if ethical relativism would submerge them in anomie, destroying the norms that had guided their lives; and if religious "lukewarmness" threatened to destroy the motivation and urgency to communicate the message to others; then the danger was mortal and a response had to be sought. Fundamentalism offered itself as a sure response, as an impregnable bastion, and as a powerful weapon in the struggle for the true faith.

C. *If there was to be a way out of this situation, the response had to arise from the very heart of evangelical piety.* That happened in two ways. One, which we shall examine more carefully in the next chapter, was the Pentecostal movement. The other, to which we will dedicate a few lines to conclude our reflection in this chapter, is what has been called the *neo-evangelical* movement, a neologism I do not like. I should prefer simply to speak of the *evangelical renewal* which, in Latin America, has been represented mainly by the Latin American Theological Fraternity, which we associate with the names of René Padilla, Peter Savage, Samuel Escobar, Pedro Arana, Emilio A. Núñez, and many others, and which has exerted an ever growing weight in the evangelical world since its origins in 1970. Without doubt it was also stimulated and nurtured by movements in other countries, particularly U.S. evangelical groups and the evangelical wing of British Anglicanism. It has, though, its own particular profile and history in our continent. I would venture to point out what I consider its most significant features:

1. It retrieved and recovered an evangelical tradition, linked especially to the Anabaptist movement of the sixteenth and seventeenth centuries and to the evangelical awakening of the eighteenth century in England and the United States (referred to earlier) both in the Reformed and in the Wesleyan tradition, but also to the origins of our own missionary Protestantism in Latin America. The work of Escobar, Arana, and Padilla shows us that this is not a mere vindication of a tradition but rather a search for elements that can fertilize theological reflection and evangelical practice for today's Latin America.

2. The movement began with an affirmation of the *centrality of Scripture,* in the twofold critique of crass literalism and the arbitrary interpretation of fundamentalism, and of a liberalism which seemed to reduce the Bible to a collection of documents from the past or a repository of religious truths and general and universal ethics. In the Cochabamba 1970 meeting it was expressed as follows:

> Assent to the authority of the Bible could be considered as one of the most general features of the evangelical movement in Latin America. . . . It can be admitted, however, that the actual use of the Bible by most Latin American evangelical people did not always coincide with the assent that distinguished it. The Bible is revered, but the voice of the Lord who speaks through it is not always obeyed. . . . We need a hermeneutic that in each case will do justice to the Biblical text. . . . The Biblical message has indisputable relevance for the Latin American person, but its proclamation does not have in our midst the place it should.[33]

Since then this work has deepened and widened, and we can see this in biblical commentaries, translations and exegeses, and in other series of important productions.

3. The Latin American affirmation opens with a criticism of Latin American Protestantism's "acculturation" to the cultural norms of the missionary-sending nations. In Lausanne, 1974, René Padilla rejected

33. "Declaración Evangélica de Cochabamba," Latin American Theological Fraternity, in *Pensamiento Cristiano,* no. 69 (March 1971): 19-21.

the identification of evangelical faith with the "American way of life."[34] In *The Gospel Today* (El Evangelio Hoy)[35] the same author stated: "Since the Word became flesh, the only possibility in regard to the communication of the Gospel is that it be incarnate in culture in order to be accessible to human beings as cultural beings."[36] Shortly thereafter, at the Willowbank "Gospel and Culture" consultation, this theme was deepened, differentiating a critical and positive dialogue with culture from a rejection or an uncritical and indiscriminate acceptance of culture.

4. Consideration of structural elements — political, economic, social — of Latin American reality could not long be put off. Samuel Escobar continued to underline the social aspects:

> The temptation for evangelicals today is to reduce the Gospel, to mutilate it, to eliminate the demand for the fruit of repentance and any aspect that would make it unpalatable to an idolatrous society. . . . Spirituality without discipleship in daily social, economic and political aspects of life is religiosity and not Christianity.[37]

The Latin American Theological Fraternity assembly in Quito in 1990, commemorating the twenty years since its foundation, summarized and reissued work done in a series of consultations of the previous years.[38] Clearly one can notice the diversity of analysis and of positions, but also the seriousness and urgency with which the task was faced. The consultations and studies on economic problems were equally valuable. The output of this work was more than evident at CLADE (Conferencia Latinoamericana de Evangelización) III in 1992, celebrated in Quito, under the theme "The Whole Gospel for All Peoples from Latin America."

5. This last meeting went beyond the limits of the Latin American Theological Fraternity to become a truly "Latin American Protestant Congress," as much due to the breadth of its representation as to the

---

34. J. .D. Douglas, ed., *Let the Earth Hear His Voice,* International Congress on World Evangelization (Minneapolis: World Wide Publications, 1975), pp. 125ff.

35. *El Evangelio Hoy* (Buenos Aires: Ed. Certeza, 1975).

36. *Let the Earth Hear His Voice,* p. 310.

37. Samuel Escobar, "Evangelism and Man's Search for Freedom, Justice, and Fulfillment," in *Let the Earth Hear His Voice,* p. 310.

38. See the 1990 issues of *Boletín Teológico* published by FTE (nos. 37, 38, 39, and 40) and the addresses and debates in the Quito meeting in issue 42-43 of September 1991.

wealth of materials and the freedom of debate. We were there present at a truly "ecumenical event" — if the reader will forgive the use of this controversial term — of Latin American Protestantism.[39]

This positive evaluation — which I feel is only just — nevertheless poses a question: Is the theological framework of the "evangelical" tradition sufficiently rich as to recover and reformulate within itself a Latin American Protestant theology? As we asked with regard to the "liberal face" of Protestantism: Might it not here be necessary to reclaim our evangelical identity, examine it critically, and attempt to surpass it positively?

---

39. The report, *CLADE III; Tercer Congreso Latinoamericano de Evangelización* (Buenos Aires: FTL, 1993), 867 pages, includes all of the preparatory materials, the addresses, the debates, and final documents of CLADE III and is the best material to evaluate the process the Fraternity has inspired and the breadth of participation obtained.

3. The Pentecostal Face of Latin American Protestantism

IN HIS FAMOUS "Seven Essays on the Peruvian Reality," Carlos Mariátegui commented in 1928:

> Protestantism is not able to penetrate Latin America by virtue of its spiritual and religious power but by its social services (YMCA, Methodist missions in the mountains, etc.). These and other signs indicate that their possibilities of normal expansion are exhausted.[1]

At that time Mariátegui was right. Protestantism had been in the region for almost a half-century; the churches had been established, but they had only been able, at the strictly religious level, to gather members in what years ago I referred to as "the loose dust on the surface of Latin American society." What the Peruvian writer could not guess was that, twenty years before, in a port city of Chile, and two years later in the growing city of Sao Paulo, a Protestantism had begun to develop that, given the social changes that began to appear just about the time he wrote, would demolish the barrier which had barred Protestantism from access to the popular masses.

The most notable of the missionaries who came to Latin America, looking back on his almost twenty years of experience in trying to reach

---

1. Carlos Mariátegui, *Siete Ensayos sobre la realidad peruana* (Lima: Amauta, 1975), pp. 172-73.

the Latin American intelligentsia with the gospel, echoed Mariátegui's diagnosis: "I am convinced that a great deal of missionary and Christian work in general has erred by the exclusive attempt to influence the 'leaders,'" and added: "No Christian movement can succeed today that does not move the masses and make them the chief objective."[2] Twenty-five years later, by now back in the United States and after a Latin America "tour," John A. Mackay — for it is he to whom we refer — would salute Pentecostal growth as a fulfillment of that 1939 vision:

> The Pentecostals had something to offer, something that brought a thrill to people benumbed by the drabness of their existence. Millions responded to the gospel. Their lives became transformed, and their horizons were widened; life took on dynamic significance. The reality of God, Jesus Christ and the Holy Spirit — previously no more than sentimental terms linked to ritual and folklore — took on new meaning, became media whereby light, strength and hope were communicated to the human spirit. People became persons, with something to live for.[3]

Meanwhile, in effect, the Pentecostal movement was well advanced in a development which was already beginning to fascinate students of religious phenomena.

All histories of Latin American Protestantism commence with the "awakening" associated with the name of missionary Willis C. Hoover, the Methodist church, and the city of Valparaiso, Chile, and continue with Luigi Francescon and the Assemblies of God in Brazil. Then Pentecostalism multiplies, diversifies, and expands, and from the 1950 decade on it becomes the popular face of Protestant Latin America.[4] Fourteen thou-

---

2. John A. Mackay, "How My Mind Has Changed in the Last Thirty Years," *Christian Century*, July 12, 1939, p. 874.

3. "Latin America and Revolution — II: 'The New Mood in the Churches,'" *Christian Century*, November 24, 1965, p. 1439.

4. Prof. Mendonça called my attention to a story in the work of Emile Léonard, *O Protestantismo Brasileiro* (Sao Paulo: ASTE, n.d.; originally published, 1951-52), pp. 56ff., of an expression of a Pentecostal nature in 1840 in the ministry of a Presbyterian missionary and a Catholic ex-priest, José Manoel de Conceicao, who subsequently would continue that ministry by himself. Léonard was possibly the first to notice what Bernardo Campos calls "pentecostality" — and which Léonard defines as "enlightenment" — in Brazilian Protestantism. Cf. his book *L'Illuminisme dans un protestantisme de constitution récente (Brésil)* (Paris: Presses Universitaires de France, 1952). "Illuminisme" does not

sand five hundred in 1938, 1 million in 1950, 37 million in 1980. Enthusiasts speak of 65 million Pentecostals by the end of the millennium.

It is not my purpose to continue this history, much less to try to "typify" the various "Pentecostalisms." We are here interested in reflecting on their piety and theology. To do so, we shall limit ourselves to what has been called the "native Pentecostalism" *(pentecostalismo criollo),* placing in parentheses the new Pentecostal currents of the last decade and the charismatic movements within the "traditional" churches. I do not mean to deny or underestimate these movements. As for the first, I believe its difference with "native Pentecostalism" is of a qualitative nature: it is within another social dynamic, related to the conditions and social stratifications generated by the application of social and economic policies of "neoconservatism," it has a different rationale, more linked to the use of media created by "technical reason" and employed "from above" upon the new conditions — very different from the popular "social creation" of native Pentecostalism. It gives rise, therefore, to another type of commitment, more tied to the "consumption of religious goods" than to active incorporation into an intentional religious subject. Hence, I believe it requires other research methods and other theological evaluation norms. That is not the case with the charismatic movements within already established churches; these, however, also are different because they arise against the background of an already established Protestant or Catholic religious practice, and generally within their parameters, and they also belong, in their majority, to middle-class sectors, with their own particular psychological and social characteristics. One hopes that a more precise and profound methodological study would lead to a better understanding of these realities of the current Latin American religious world.[5]

---

refer in Léonard's work to the cultural movement we usually call "enlightenment." In this sense it was used in sixteenth-century Spain for a mystic movement, "los iluminados," and refers to a form of "mystical" experience of the Spirit.

5. There have been several efforts to categorize Latin American "Pentecostalisms" or to elaborate what Petersen has called the "taxonomies of Latin American Pentecostalism." Prof. Antonio Gouvea Mendonça distinguishes "classical" Pentecostalism and "neopentecostalism," and within the latter between an "autonomous" Pentecostalism and a "healing" Pentecostalism. Bishop Manuel Gaxiola-Gaxiola, of the United Pentecostal Mexican Church, speaks of different groupings of Pentecostal churches: autochthonous, denominations founded by foreign churches, and a special type of church similar to the messianic-prophetic independent churches of Africa ("Latin American Pentecostalism:

I. What Does Pentecostalism Represent within Latin American Protestantism?

Contrary to what we have done in previous situations, I do not think it adequate to begin with the foreign "roots" of Pentecostalism. That is not to deny them — we shall return to that in the second section of this chapter. However, to begin at that point would obscure the nature of the phenomenon we wish to understand. No doubt the contact Pastor Hoover had with the early North American Pentecostal manifestations had its importance — interestingly, by means of a little book sent to the missionary's wife from India by a woman missionary friend who had discovered there the movement which originated in California just four years earlier. Also, the history of the Waldensian Italian Luigi Frances- con, who had received the baptism of the Spirit in an Italian-language Baptist congregation in Chicago in 1907 and came to Argentina and Brazil in 1910 as the result of a vision. What these "triggers" did, how- ever, was only to "awaken" a religious experience already latent in Latin American popular sectors. The seed could have been sown in Los An- geles or Chicago, but it was planted in Latin American soil, it fed on the vital juices of this land, and the new Latin American popular masses proved that the taste of the fruit met the demands of their palate.

A Mosaic within a Mosaic," *Pneuma* 13, no. 2 [fall 1991]: 107ff.). The first, in his opinion, were born with scant or no foreign influence, and their practices arose directly from the traditions of the people where they appeared. Carmelo Alvarez, from his perspective, also distinguishes between "native Pentecostalism" with some historic rootage in Latin America and churches more recently planted by foreign missions, which he associates with the "electronic church" and with evangelists such as Jimmy Swaggart ("Latin American Pentecostals: Ecumenical and Evangelicals," *Catholic Ecumenical Review* 23, no. 1-2 [October 1986]: 93ff.). We shall make some observations in this regard in the last chapter. The strong ideological coloring of many of these movements, tied directly or indirectly to "the new religious right" in the United States, should also be kept in mind. See in this connection the work of Erling Jorstad, *The Politics of Moralism: The New Christian Right in American Life* (Minneapolis: Augsburg, 1981), and above all his ample investigation and analysis in *The New Christian Right: 1981-1988*, Studies in American Religion, vol. 25 (Lewiston/Queenston: Edwin Mellen Press, 1987). In his unpublished thesis Douglas Petersen questions taxonomies based on "origin" — local or of foreign missions — because what matters is not the historic origin but rather the measure of effective "indigenization" they have reached. It seems clear that we still lack criteria that allow us a more adequate typology. Also, the highly dynamic character of the entire process renders difficult the definition of such criteria.

Francescon, Hoover, or Berg may have spoken with a foreign accent, but the "language of the Spirit" they uttered found an echo in the dockworkers of Valparaiso and the laborers of São Paulo, and it was repeated in the languages of Chilean "rotos," Toba and Aymara indigenous peoples, and Central American peasants.

A. Latin American Protestantism did not take notice of what was happening until the Pentecostal congregations began to multiply in their neighborhoods. For "evangelical" Protestantism they represented a challenge and a temptation. They could recognize their own theology, their ethical views, and their evangelistic zeal in the Pentecostals, but their manifestations were strange to them and their growth both frightened and seduced them. Some entrenched themselves in their denominational identity and rejected them, others were enthusiastic and emulated them. Conflicts arose and in some cases ruptures. Baptists and Free Brethren suffered these tensions most acutely, but they were present as well among Methodists, Presbyterians, and the Disciples of Christ.

B. For "liberal" Protestantism the matter was even more difficult. The first reaction was decidedly negative. The Methodist Church of Chile resolved it drastically on September 12, 1909: Hoover and his followers were expelled from the Methodist church and the teachings and practices of their movement were rejected as "anti-Methodist, contrary to the Scriptures and irrational." "At that time" — Hollenweger commented — "Methodists confirmed law and order but lost the heart of the people. The [Chilean] Pentecostals celebrate the 12th of September as the anniversary of their reformation."[6] Time would smooth out the rough spots, but for many years the verdict would continue to be the same.

When the Methodist church stated that Pentecostalism was "irrational," however, it posed a problem that required an answer. On the basis of what rationality is such a judgment made? Is it possible that there may be a "rationality" that allows one to understand what was happening? A new generation of "liberal Protestantism" began to try to respond to these questions. Its tools to do so were born of the same modern rationalism that had raised the accusation; the response was sought in social sciences.

C. From this perspective a series of diverse hypotheses arose, but with a common denominator: They saw Pentecostalism as a movement

6. Walter Hollenweger, in *Spiritus: Studies on Pentecostalism,* year 1, no. 1 (1985).

which found its space in Latin America's transition from a traditional society to a modern one, or more specifically, in the transition from a largely agrarian society to a partially industrialized one, from a rural to an urban society. Pentecostalism's entrance into this area was seen in various ways. Though this is not our central point of concentration, it is well to review rapidly some of the more characteristic theses.

Though there are earlier studies, it is curious that three Protestants — two Swiss and a Brazilian of German origin — were the first to attempt an in-depth analysis of the Pentecostal phenomenon. One, a historian, Professor Walter Hollenweger,[7] saw it as a typical phenomenon of the culture of the popular classes: It is an oral religion expressed in symbols (song, dance), an emotional and preconceptual religion, from which one cannot expect an explicit and systematic theology. The perspective employed corresponds to a vision for which there is a kind of "progress" from primitive stages, inarticulate and primary, to others more evolved, characterized by written language, which were capable of abstraction and systematization. There is some truth in this theory; it would seem, in effect, that as much at the level of individual psychic development as at that of societies, the processes of abstraction, conceptualization, and systematization require time to develop. Often, however, these theories reveal certain prejudices: that what is at stake is an advance from "inferior" modes of knowledge, which are surpassed by others that are "superior"; that the latter are more "profound" or richer than the former; that "abstraction" captures the realities it refers to with more precision. We are then surprised when "developed" cultures "regress" to manifestations they find more satisfactory, more "complete," more expressive.[8]

The two sociologists, Emilio Willems and Christian Lalive d'Epinay, studied Chilean and Brazilian Pentecostalism following a Weberian outline: Pentecostalism functions as an escape, or a way to respond to personal and collective crises unleashed by the shift from a traditional rural culture to one that is urban, industrial, and democratic. For Wil-

7. There are many publications of Professor Hollenweger, beginning with his monumental thesis in eight volumes, *Handbuch der Pfingstbewegung* (Geneva: World Council of Churches, 1965), mimeographed. The references we use are found in Walter Hollenweger, *The Pentecostals* (Minneapolis: Augsburg, 1972).

8. In more recent publications Hollenweger has revised and amplified his initial thesis. See, for example, "Twenty Years After," in *Spiritus: Studies on Pentecostalism,* Mexico, year 2, no. 1 (1986). Reproduced in Juan Sepúlveda, ed., *Antología sobre Pentecostalismo* (Santiago, Chile, 1989).

lems[9] Pentecostalism paves a way of transition toward a new identity, form of life, and social structure, thus allowing the believers to enter successfully into modern society and to adapt to it.[10] For Lalive d'Epinay,[11] on the other hand, what Pentecostalism offers is a "refuge" which, while allowing the believers to live in the new society, "protects" them, re-creating in the ecclesial community a kind of "remedial" traditional society. For both, the new "identity" given by conversion and the open leadership, which is not legitimated professionally but by the personal charisma and the face-to-face solidarity of the Pentecostal community, are the new factors which make Pentecostalism a religiosity adequate to meet the condition of "anomie" produced by the change.

The Brazilian sociologist Francisco Cartaxo Rolim[12] builds also on the basis of social transition, but he criticizes his predecessors at two points. The first is that they are concerned more with "what Pentecostalism does" than with "what Pentecostalism is," that is, a religious movement and hence planted in the symbolic realm in the search for meaning. The second is that the transition in society should not be seen mainly as one from agrarian to urban, from traditional to modern society, but rather as a transition from one economic system to another, specifically, to dependent capitalism. Therefore, the problem has to do with class conflict. Following a Marxist line, Rolim presupposes that the identity of social sectors only is built in relation to one's place in the social structure. Thus Pentecostalism is part of a self-identity characteristic of an "indefinite class" placed between the middle class and the workers,[13] and of necessity carrying an ambiguous self-consciousness. For that reason, he concludes, when one compares it to ecclesial base

9. Emilio Willems, *Followers of the New Faith* (Nashville: Vanderbilt University Press, 1967). By the same author, "Religious Mass Movements and Social Change in Brazil," in *New Perspectives on Brazil,* ed. E. N. Baklanoff (1966).

10. Recently the British sociologist David Martin has again taken up the same thesis, with some variations, in his book *Tongues of Fire,* 2d ed. (New York: Basil Blackwell, 1991), which, strangely, has been celebrated in the Anglo-Saxon world as a "discovery" but in which the information, knowledge of Latin America, and methodology seem to us to leave much to be desired.

11. Christian Lalive d'Epinay, *Haven of the Masses: A Study of the Pentecostal Movement in Chile* (London: Lutterworth Press, 1969). By the same author, various articles (cited in the bibliography of the book mentioned) and *Religion, Dynamique Social et Dependence* (Paris: Mouton, 1975).

12. *Pentecostais no Brasil* (Petropolis: Editorial Vozes, 1985).

13. Ibid., p. 15.

communities (CEBs), that while Pentecostalism displaces the claim for social justice to the spiritual world (because it is not firmly embedded in the working-class world), the CEBs create a social conscience because they are a class "in and for itself." Though this proposition is very debatable, Rolim's approach has the value of seeing Pentecostalism not only as part of a social dynamic, but as a structure of meaning, as a specifically religious phenomenon. It also attempts to define its theology — which, of course, he calls "Pentecostal ideology" — and recognizes the measure of "continuity" that exists between that religiosity and traditional Latin American religiosity.

Again, we must ask ourselves if these are adequate presuppositions to understand a religious reality. It is reasonable to think that one's place in the social structure may influence the nature of religious phenomena, but is this so to the extent Rolim supposes? Even along this same line, the work of Néstor García Canclini allows a further advance. On the one hand, if it is true that the understandings of a given social sector try to harmonize their vision of reality with the objective conditions that surround it, it is also true that it is not a matter of "frozen" visions but of dynamic processes in which each sector struggles to impose a worldview that has to do not only with its structural situation but also with its traditions — in this case its religious traditions — and with other elements: "what man imagines beyond his material conditions."[14] Then, "it is reasonable to think . . . that we should consider the possibility of the existence of other aspects of human life (conflictive or not) which find expression through religious channels: fear of death or of sickness, sense of guilt, search for a transcendent meaning to life."[15] In this direction studies begin to appear that seek a hermeneutical key to the Pentecostal symbolic system using the writing of as diverse a group of authors as Ricoeur, Cassirer, Bourdieu, or Luckmann.

One should not forget that all these essays share one location in common: they look at Pentecostalism "from outside." Even a "participant observer" — as Lalive d'Epinay describes himself — continues to enjoy the "advantage" of an "observer," which might guarantee greater objectivity, but also suffers from its limitation — the difficult access to

14. *Las culturas populares en el Capitalismo* (Mexico City: Editorial Nueva Imagen, 1983), p. 22; ET, *Transforming Modernity in Mexico: Popular Culture in Mexico* (Austin: University of Texas Press, 1993).

15. Daniel P. Míguez, *Estilos de Vida e Identidades,* manuscript, 1993.

the data of a subjectivity he does not share and which is the very heart of what he studies. Hence it is not surprising that Pentecostals regard these studies doubtfully. On the one hand they see themselves in the descriptions of their social reality; on the other, they feel that what is decisive and vital to them has not been taken into account.

A second or third generation of Pentecostals, which knows well the categories of the studies already done and does not reject some of their hypotheses, has begun to elaborate "from within" a more profound understanding of the Pentecostal experience. Two recent publications seem to me particularly valuable in this regard: the research of the Chilean team supported by Servicio Evangélico para el Desarrollo (SEPADE) and published in two volumes under the suggestive title *In a Strange Land*,[16] and the materials from the Latin American Pentecostal meeting in Chile in 1990.[17] Before referring to them, however, I should like to pose the issue of "normative Pentecostal theology," which will allow us — in this final section — to enter a dialogue with these new efforts.

II. Pentecostal Theology

A. *Is there a Pentecostal theology?* Although almost all authors warn that one must have in mind theological variants that exist within Pentecostalism, most coincide in a theological framework the backbone of which centers on four themes.

Salvation, by the grace of God won by the vicarious death of Jesus Christ — the redemptive blood — and received by faith. Here what is central is *experience* of conversion, for although grace is free and for all, personal experience of that grace, often but not always associated with a dramatic conversion biographically identifiable, is what grants personal reality to salvation.[18]

---

16. Santiago de Chile: Editorial Amerinda, vol. 1, 1988; vol. 2, 1991.

17. Carmelo Alvarez, ed., *Pentecostalismo y Liberación* (San José, Costa Rica: Ediciones DEI, 1992); ET forthcoming.

18. As a curious exception to this "universality of grace," one must mention the "Igreja de Deus" in Brazil, Presbyterian in origin, which adheres firmly to the doctrine of double predestination and therefore makes no effort to proselytize or to "convert people" but simply receives those who come and "witness" to their election. Despite that, it is a church which has grown in an extraordinary way, and still continues growing.

The baptism of the Holy Spirit, interpreted as a "second experience," witnessed by the "gift of tongues" which is linked to sanctification, sometimes understood as a growth process and at other times as a divine gift imparted in a unique and definitive experience. Though not all Pentecostals give the same weight to the "gift of tongues," "to receive power" is central to baptism of, or "in," the Spirit.

Divine healing as a promise for all believers, which becomes real in the community of the church, habitually by means of prayer and the laying on of hands. One has to recognize that the emphasis on healing is not the same in all branches of Pentecostalism.[19]

An apocalyptic eschatology, almost always premillenarian, the sub-themes of which tend to be: resurrection, the second coming and the millennial kingdom, judgment and the eternal kingdom.

This outline does not mean that other classic doctrines of the faith are denied. Some doctrinal declarations include the inspiration of the Scripture (Assemblies of God, 1949), sometimes referred to as "verbal" (Church of God of Cleveland), the doctrines of God and the Trinity and a Chalcedonian Christology (Church of God of Cleveland and Assemblies), baptism (normally of believers), and the church. But what Donald Dayton calls the "fourfold pattern" — "Christ the Savior, Sanctifier, Healer and coming King" — seems adequately to represent the common tradition of Pentecostalism.[20]

B. This summary must be included in the context of what was indicated in the previous chapter on the "awakenings" in the United

---

19. The almost exclusive emphasis on "divine cure" or "healing" characterizes some more recent Pentecostal movements and the "neopentecostalism" to which we referred in note 5. In this connection I think some observations of Prof. Mendonça on the preponderance of the theme of "the spirits" in this neopentecostalism of divine healing are of great interest. He considers that this tendency, introduced by missionaries of the "Four Square Gospel" around 1950, produces an "imbalance in classical Pentecostalism," in that it takes on the popular social understanding of a world governed by good and evil spirits and proposes a way of "managing" the spirit world, restricted to those who have supernatural (magical?) power. What happens here is that the gospel contents are shifted: sin is demon possession, liberation comes through exorcism, often the "control" of the spirits utilizes "tools" — blessed keys, touching an object. The church here is not mainly the congregation of committed believers. Are we here — Mendonça asks — dealing with a "new religion"? One might also see here, having in mind the Afro-American background, a manifestation of syncretism.

20. *The Theological Roots of Pentecostalism* (Grand Rapids: Francis Asbury Press, 1987), pp. 21f.

States in the second half of the nineteenth century, for there it was that the spark of Pentecostal awakening was lit. Indeed, all theology of the North American awakening should be interpreted in the framework of a "Spirit theology" that moves, so to say, in three stages that to a large degree go together: *conversion* subjectively appropriated by the operation of the Holy Spirit in salvation; *sanctification* as a "second blessing" — be it sudden or gradual, complete or growing — sometimes called the "baptism of the Spirit"; and a *"fullness of the Spirit"* or "receiving the power of the Spirit," associated in Pentecostalism with the gift of tongues and other ecstatic manifestations (sometimes considered a "third blessing" and at other times identified as part of the second).

Usually the beginnings of Pentecostalism are linked with the events related to the ministry of the black pastor William Seymour in the Azusa Street hall in Los Angeles in 1906. In his classic work *The Holiness-Pentecostal Movement in the United States,*[21] V. Synan describes this theology as "Arminian, perfectionist, premillennial and charismatic."

This interpretation, however, has been criticized by those who see a double origin,[22] one component being more closely tied to the Reformed and Baptist traditions and the other to the Wesleyan holiness stream. Following these interpretations, Pastor Douglas Peterson, missionary of the Assemblies of God in Costa Rica, maintained in his doctoral thesis that one should speak of two currents that converge in the movement: the Wesleyan holiness tradition and the premillennial and dispensationalist line of the Keswick Conferences and of the "Prophecy Conferences" (mentioned earlier) as contained within the movements of Moody, Torrey, and other evangelists. The "recovery" of the gift of tongues, whose long tradition is well known and which had manifestations in the awakenings of the second half of the nineteenth century, became a distinctive element of Pentecostalism since the ministry of Charles Fox Parham in Topeka, Kansas (from which Seymour, a lay evangelist, separated, in part due to the racist tendencies of Parham), and the tradition of "empowerment" related to evangelization, healing, and miracles more linked to the Keswick line and which is

---

21. Grand Rapids: Eerdmans, 1971, p. 217.

22. Robert M. Anderson, *The Vision of the Disinherited: The Making of American Pentecostalism* (New York: Oxford University Press, 1979), chapter on "The Message of Pentecostalism."

equally received in some streams of Pentecostal development. The convergence of these two currents has not meant that the difference of emphases between them has disappeared.

C. The later rapid development, as much in California itself as in the East and in the Baptist churches of Chicago, soon gave rise to a variety of churches, whether among those already present in the holiness movement that take on Pentecostalism, or in new ones that were born. This is the theological tradition of the various Pentecostal churches that entered Latin America in the first half of this century.

III. A Latin American Pentecostal Theology?

A. The work of Sepúlveda and Campos, mentioned previously, seeks a theological expression which will spring from the Latin American Pentecostal experience itself. Thus Sepúlveda describes the Pentecostal theology of the early Chilean experience (1910-60) "in the context of exclusion," whose main themes would be as follows: (1) A Manichean view of the world (Spirit vs. matter, heaven vs. earth, church vs. world, believer vs. Gentile, God vs. the devil, good vs. evil, and soul vs. body) radicalized due to "a real experience of the negativity and brutality of the world." "When a Pentecostal says: 'this world offers nothing, it only offers perdition' ('perdición' means both lostness and damnation) he/she is not stating a dogmatic affirmation but rather is relating or giving voice to his/her own experience" (misery, unemployment, illness, alcoholism, etc.). (2) "Determinism and anthropological pessimism," respectively, would describe the experience of the "old man," incapable of freeing himself from certain "vices" and the feeling of impotence in the face of objective forces that cannot be dominated, personified in Satan and the demons. (3) The affirmation of "the power of the Holy Spirit" does not correspond in Chilean Pentecostalism, differing from the North American one, to a doctrine and a codification but to a recognition of the work of the Spirit in "multiple manifestations . . . from angelic tongues to simple joy, including dance, visions, etc.," "the certainty of the nearness and living presence of a forgiving and accepting God." "It is a form of social and popular reappropriation of the power of God in the face of its sacramental appropriation by the Catholic Church and its rationalistic appropriation in the preaching of historical Protestantism." (4) Equally, in contrast with the appropriation of the Bible by the "religious profession-als," for Pentecostals "all mediation between the believer and the Bible disappears except for the illumination and inspiration of the Holy Spirit"; each believer can own his or her own Bible, read it, understand it, and preach it. (5) Finally, there is a "Church militant" into which one enters by conversion and to which one subordinates personal interests, in which one participates fully and with which a total commitment is taken.[23]

B. *Is this theology sufficient?* Surely no one who has related even minimally to Pentecostal persons and congregations will dispute the correctness of this interpretation. Sepúlveda, nevertheless, wants to pose the question about how native Pentecostalism can evolve theologically given the changes taking place in society (in his case, Chile, which underwent a time of social opening between 1964-73 and the dictatorship of 1973-85). The Pentecostal does not now feel that he/she is "excluded" from a world dominated by Satan but rather sees himself/herself as a possible participant in democratic changes that improve everyone's situation or as excluded by historical factors (the dictatorship) that can be concretely identified. Those who thus perceive things begin to read the Bible with different eyes: they see Christian militancy differently, they seek their "Pentecostal identity" in other terms. But, at the same time, this change implies a certain "ideological mediation" in which many fear the loss of their Protestant identity and others find the defense of the "status quo" as the only possible stance and hence lean toward ways of social and political participation that will assure it (whereby, in effect, they also take on an ideological mediation of another kind).

Probably it is pertinent to ask to what extent these ideological options are the result of the general experience of the Pentecostal people — as Sepúlveda seems to believe — or ideological options of some leaders, not necessarily assumed by the majority. The results of plebiscites and elections in areas with a significant Pentecostal presence seem to suggest that the options of the leadership, which are followed on the religious plane, are not always taken up at the political level. This suspicion can be verified in "political" experiences of Pentecostal leaders in other Latin American nations. This observation, however, does not invalidate the fundamental affirmation of Sepúlveda with regard to the

---

23. "Pentecostal Theology in the Context of the Struggle for Life," in *Faith Born in the Struggle for Life*, ed. D. Kirkpatrick (Grand Rapids: Eerdmans, 1988), pp. 299ff.

evolution of the Pentecostal conscience, from a mainly symbolic plane to a more historical one.

It is possible to identify at least three ways in which this step toward a greater social and political participation finds expression. At certain points these three forms coincide, but in others they contradict each other.

1. On the one hand, it is clear that Pentecostal churches have developed a social conscience expressed in "service to the most needy," not just at a personal and occasional level but in an institutionalized form, and not only for church members but for the surrounding community. The Assemblies of God have created a Childcare Service Program in Central American countries. A number of local Pentecostal churches offer social, medical, and juridical assistance — at times somewhat resisted by traditional pastors or groups. Parish schools or remedial education centers are also signs of an institutional advance and a more reflective sense of social responsibility.

2. Secondly, several Latin American Pentecostal churches — of course not all of them — have organized a series of consultations trying to articulate, from their own Pentecostal experience and understandings, some ethical convictions with reference to society, a kind of "social creed project." The Encounter of Latin American Pentecostals celebrated in Salvador (Bahia, Brazil) in January 1988 noted that:

> Pentecostal experiences narrated by the presenters and shared by all the groups allowed us to recognize as a new fact, and already with considerable force in the Pentecostal universe, the emergence of Pentecostal churches which, surpassing a historical tendency to social marginalization, have been committing themselves to those who suffer and discovering new forms of social engagement.[24]

The following meeting took place in Santiago de Chile in December 1990 under the theme "Pentecostalism and Liberation" with the purpose "to create a place to debate problems, challenges and contributions of the Pentecostal movement in the Latin American context."[25] Two par-

---

24. "Documento de Síntesis" (mimeographed), from Encuentro de Pentecostales Latinoamericanos, in Salvador, Bahia, Brazil, January 6-9, 1988, p. 5.

25. This and other quotes from this meeting are taken from its "Final Document," published in Carmelo Alvarez, ed., *Pentecostalismo y liberación* (San José, Costa Rica: DEI, 1992), pp. 252-54; ET forthcoming.

agraphs seem to me significant to summarize this new awareness of the place of social responsibility in the Pentecostal movement:

> The Pentecostal movement is present, in the main, among the poorer sectors of our rural and urban areas. From the reality, *which was also the reality from which Jesus carried out his ministry* (Luke 4:18), Pentecostalism challenges *a sinful society* which is in frank decay. At the same time it is challenged by the need for justice and restoration of our peoples, where is very evident the marginalization of women, aborigines, blacks, young people. These challenges are given hopeful answers, but *often also escapist answers*. (p. 253)

> We reaffirm our conviction regarding the work of the Holy Spirit, manifested in various gifts; in faith experiences that impact personal life, community life and all of creation, transforming them and filling them with the fullness of God. Fullness which is shown in the multiform grace of the Lord, *in liberating actions of the Spirit which demolish sinful structures of destruction, misery and death vanquished by Jesus Christ;* in the powerful testimonies of women and men who in the church *and beyond it* struggle and work for "the abundant life" promise of Jesus, with the poor, the sad, those who have no succour, the oppressed. (p. 154)

I have taken the freedom of italicizing some phrases which, among others, point to a significant deepening of theological conscience: a reading of the Bible that goes beyond the literal to a merging — which in practice Pentecostals already carry out — of the social horizon of the text and their own; a vision of a society that takes account of the structural aspects of human life — oppression, discrimination, social decay — and sees in them an area for the work of the Spirit; and hence the awareness that in this space — outside the church — there is a genuine evangelical vocation.

3. Alongside these service activities and these reflections at a social and theological level there developed, often without much contact with them, the "political activity" of Pentecostal leaders which has drawn the attention of nonbelieving observers. Known examples are those of Peru in recent elections, of evangelical members of Congress in Brazil, of attempts to create Protestant political parties in Argentina, and other less known cases of elections of local and municipal authorities and of functionaries in jobs with political import, not to speak of the evangel-

ical presence in the life and political struggles of Central America — all constitutive of a new reality that we cannot exclude from our analysis.[26]

Observations that come to me from personal contacts, generally occasional and somewhat superficial, suggest that, in most cases, there is not conscious linkage between faith professed and political activity, except in the very general affirmation of "doing good" or "wanting to help" and the possibilities of evangelization — for example, introducing the reading of the Bible and prayer to the realm of political life, or working for favorable conditions for the church, including protection of religious liberty. It is not that these motivations are not genuine and, to a degree, legitimate. However, the absence of a mediating ethical-social thought structure and of an analytical-critical understanding of the political sphere can easily betray the honesty of the persons who participate (for instance, by being co-opted by ideological options the social consequences of which they do not perceive) or seduce the participants to settle for a "theocratic" use of the — generally quite limited — power derived from this participation.

On the other hand, the lack of experience of those who take up these activities — often pastors whose local popularity results from their religious leadership or their benevolence activity — makes them very vulnerable to temptations to power or the "snares" of client-seeking politicians. Perhaps it would be desirable that the growing social conscience of these and other Protestant communities, which generally have been absent from political activity, be channeled to participation in "social movements" — neighborhood associations, consumer groups, ecology movements, human rights groups, school or hospital cooperative associations, or many other forms of social participation at local and national levels. First, the aims and purposes of these are more

26. There are still few wide-ranging and reliable studies of this activity and of its theological and social significance. The few we have in hand refer to "evangelicals" in general. For example: David Stoll, *Is Latin America Turning Protestant? The Politics of Evangelical Growth* (Berkeley: University of California Press, 1990) and *Rethinking Protestantism in Latin America* (Philadelphia: Temple University Press, 1993); René Padilla, *De la marginalidad al Compromiso: los evangélicos y la política en América Latina* (Buenos Aires: Fraternidad Teológica Latinoamericana, 1990); Fortunato Mallimaci, *Protestantismo y política partidaria actual en Argentina: Del campo religioso al campo político, la lucha por la legitimidad* (mimeographed) (Buenos Aires, 1994), 22 pages; Paul Freston, *Teócratas, Fisiológicos, Nova Direita y Progresistas: Protestantes e Politica na Nova Republica* (Rio de Janeiro: CEDI, 1989).

limited and specifically defined, and believers can participate in them with greater confidence; secondly, relationships are more personal, face-to-face, more in line with what they are accustomed to in the ecclesial community; and finally there is less corruption and the struggle for power is less violent. In this regard, participants can obtain "training" while at the same time contributing to public life. The more modern constitutions of our countries are beginning to include different indirect participation possibilities in political life, through which Protestants can begin to channel their social conscience. To be sure, this does not replace nor reduce the importance and necessity of political life in the more strict sense and in political party involvement, but perhaps it offers a space where specific political vocations can be awakened and developed.

C. It is clear that not all Pentecostalism, not even all "native Pente-costalism," shares this new conscience nor opens itself spontaneously to social and political activity. It is clear also that here we have the expressions of the Pentecostal leadership. But the question remains whether the churches that have moved in this direction, and the leaders who express it, are "stating explicitly" a true development of religious awareness and are expressing the social aspirations of Pentecostal people, or on the contrary, are introducing a "shock" that will result in an internal crisis or will conspire against the continuity of growth that has characterized Pentecostalism.

The problem is real but not easily resolved. *Are we, in the end, before a thriving, growing Pentecostalism, but threatened by the same social factors that make its development possible?* This is not just a rhetorical question when we observe the social and political options of important Pentecostal sectors in Chile, Peru, Brazil, or Guatemala. It would seem that Pentecostalism, by becoming a central actor in the religious field, faces decisions in which it will no longer be able to perpetuate a life solely based on the experience of salvation under the conditions of its origin. It may be that many Pentecostals are poor or marginalized, but as a whole they represent now a social and political force. Thus both the context of their experience and hence of its implicit contents is change.

In an excellent article — which, out of respect for its complexity and richness, I exempt myself from summarizing — Bernardo Campos develops, with a theoretical framework unlike Sepúlveda's, a similar thesis: The exclusion of which the Pentecostal is victim is transformed into a positive factor because it allows the person to break with the "sense" of "the official socio-production" and "create his/her own meaning."

> In this way, the rupture of one sense simultaneously leads to the creation — recomposition — of another. It is a craft with which the Pentecostal community produces (reconstructs) the world, re-creating itself.[27]

So far so good, but a bit further on Campos continues:

> Thus the Pentecostal community articulates a world view, with the elements available at the moment. *It does not matter if those elements are already identified with modes of knowing or modes of acting rooted in Catholic or Protestant religious structures, if they belong to . . . ancestral ideologies from their old social world . . . or if they are alien to their national production.*[28]

Is it correct that in this reconstruction the modes of knowing and acting that are already part of prior baggage of those doing the reconstructing "do not matter"? Is not the very religious experience — Pentecostal or any other — conditioned by that "baggage"? In relation to the Pentecostal movement, several observers have noted apparent "paradoxes and contradictions." For example, André Droogers points to some of these paradoxes:[29]

1. Pentecostal faith rehabilitates the laity by means of the gifts of the Holy Spirit. However, there are churches with a strong stratification and definition of power.
2. There is ample possibility for emotional expression in a context of a rigid direction with a fundamentalist scheme.
3. Pentecostals reject this world and withdraw from it, but at the same time they are seen as exemplary citizens and workers.
4. Believers avoid politics . . . however, some authors see in Pentecostal churches a social protest, and currently some churches actively intervene in politics and others emerge as a holy alternative to communism.

---

27. "Lo testimonial: un caso de teología oral y narrativa," in *Pentecostalismo y Liberación*, p. 128.

28. Ibid., p. 129, emphasis mine.

29. In *Algo Mas que Opio* (San José, Costa Rica: DEI, 1991), p. 26; ET forthcoming.

5. People seem to reject society and await the coming of Christ, but they are committed to society here and now.
6. Charismatic movements insist that people be of the same church, but the congregations maintain an ample autonomy.
7. Women occupy a central role in congregational life, but formally their subordinate position is justified, Bible in hand.

At a purely empirical level, some of these "paradoxes" should be examined with care. To mention just two examples: With reference to the final one, referring to the place of women in the Pentecostal community, it is interesting to take account of the dissertation of Elizabeth Brusco, which shows how the modification of "machista" conduct, even without modifying the symbol of feminine subordination, in fact changes the practice of the relationship and hence the self-valuation and the self-consciousness of women.[30] The other "paradox" would require a lengthier development: it involves the relationship between lay participation in the Pentecostal community and the marked hierarchical structure that grants almost total power to the leaders. This topic would lead us to a discussion of the concept of "power," on which at the moment we cannot embark. It would be interesting, however, to take account of two observations Bourdieu places in tension as he studies the matter of "power." On the one hand, he affirms that

> The concentration of political capital in the hands of a small number of persons is something that is prevented with greater difficulty — and thus all the more likely to happen — the more completely ordinary individuals are divested of the material and cultural instruments necessary for them to participate actively in politics, that is, *leisure time* and *cultural capital.*

On the other hand, he recognizes that

> This structural coincidence of the specific interest of the delegates and the interests of the mandators is the basis of the miracle of a

---

30. Elizabeth Brusco, *The Reformation of Machismo: Evangelical Conversion in Colombia* (Austin: University of Texas Press, 1995). Licenciate Mónica Tarducci presented a study at the University of Buenos Aires on the same theme under the title of "Servir al marido como al Señor: Las mujeres pentecostales" (Serving your husband as you serve the Lord: pentecostal women).

sincere and successful ministry. The people who serve the interests of
their mandators well are those who serve their own interests well by
serving others. . . .

Though Bourdieu refers here to political power, his observations are, as
he himself says, relevant — *mutatis mutandis* — also in the religious
sphere.[31] In this regard Lalive d'Epinay already called attention to the
fact that though ministerial power was exercised in the Pentecostal world
in a traditional authoritarian mode, access depended on the "charisma,"
that is, the possibility that the leader be capable of promoting and
interpreting the common religious experience.

D. *Open questions for theological reflection.* The problem posed by
the "paradoxes" is, in reality, more profound and has to do with the
relation between the "lineal logic" and "enlightened" rationality which
we usually take for granted, and the rationality of the symbolic, which
includes multiple aspects that at times come much closer to "the rationality of life" as it is experienced by the people. To pretend to reduce
the latter to the former runs the grave risk of "sterilizing" the experience.

In the conversation following the lectures which gave rise to this
book, Bernardo Campos set forth the problem in terms that contribute
to our reflection. He defines "pentecostality" as a "religious category"
that appears, at least throughout the entire Christian history, as an
immediate and transforming "spiritual experience" (an "ecstatic experience"), whose first "logos" — its first intellectual articulation — is "the
testimony," a narrative story that is expressed in the worship service and
"finds a first rationalization in public preaching, in apologetic statement
or in prayer (contemplative experience)." From there comes a transition
to the ethical formulation or the dogmatic confession and theological
articulation.[32] Pentecostalism, in a particular historical situation, in this
case that of Latin American societies, lives out this experience and
expresses it in life and worship. The "theorizing" process is barely in-
choate. Thus emerges a certain "schizophrenia" between experience and
"inherited" theology. Transition to its own articulation takes time.

Despite these clarifications, I think Sepúlveda's observation about
the problem of transition and our critique of Campos's resolution are

31. Pierre Bourdieu, *Language and Symbolic Power* (Cambridge: Cambridge Polity
Press, 1991), pp. 173, 215.
32. "Lo testimonial," p. 126 (see note 27 above).

still valid. In fact, an important branch of Pentecostalism finds itself obliged to "reconceptualize" the symbols to which it has given new meaning. That theological reconceptualization, though always dangerous, for it can enervate the symbol's dynamic, is not indifferent to but rather feeds back into the significance of the symbol. In other words, *the symbol may have various meanings, but if it turns out to be absurd or contradictory with regard to its new "meaning," sooner or later it ends up being cast away.* In this sense, the need remains for the Pentecostal movement to examine its "explicit" theology in terms of the "implicit" theology in its foundational experience.

These remarks are certainly not meant as a criticism of Pentecostalism. As a matter of fact, my observations apply to a greater or lesser degree to all Latin American evangelical Protestantism — and perhaps not to it alone. Even less is it an invitation to blur its profile or to "moderate" the intensity of its experience. Precisely because Pentecostalism quantitatively is the most significant manifestation, and qualitatively the most vigorous expression, of Latin American Protestantism, its future is decisive not only for Protestantism as a whole but for the entire religious field and its social projection. In this sense I am not the first to remark that the theological clothing that Latin American Pentecostalism inherited is too tight to fit its experience or to allow free expression of its vigor. It is to be desired that this very experience may free itself of some inherited distortions and find a theological language that will explore the riches of the Spirit experience and thus surpass the contradictions that frequently are noted between its religious experience, its ecclesial vigor, its conscience of solidarity, and its popular belonging, and the language and theological structure that attempts to frame and express them.

There are two aspects of this need for revision that seem central to me, for it is in them that the conceptualization in which the symbol was taken up seems to so contradict the real experience and practice of the great majority of the current Pentecostal movement that it threatens to provoke a crisis of faith in new Pentecostal generations. I refer to biblical fundamentalism and premillennial apocalypticism.

1. "Slavery to the letter and the freedom of the Spirit." We have repeatedly underlined the centrality of Scripture in Pentecostal life — indeed in all Latin American evangelicalism. The Bible is a sign of identification when going to church with it under one's arm; it is a "defensive weapon" when others mock or disqualify that faith, and of "conquest"

when one witnesses and seals it with "God says it in his Word"; it is the response to dilemmas when it is opened "without looking" and the text which "leaps out" responds to a need or an immediate problem; it is what provides a "language" to praise the Lord, to pray, to offer testimony.

What happens, however, when one attempts to express conceptually "what it is" and "how to understand" that Scripture? All Pentecostal doctrinal documents that I am aware of affirm without doubt the principle of *sola scriptura*: not a few add a word about "verbal inspiration," "infallibility," or "the infallible inspired Word of God." Teaching along these lines in most Pentecostal seminaries adopts a fundamentalist interpretation of the "literal sense" of the texts and in many cases follows the dispensationalist hermeneutic of Scofield's Bible. Generally, when a Pentecostal explains why the Bible is the Word of God, those are the reasons given . . . even when often the "explanation" culminates with a reference to how he or she "found in the Bible the message of life and salvation," or "how God spoke to" him or her.

Placing the fundamentalist conception that expresses doctrinally the meaning of Scripture side by side with the life experience of it and the interpretation of texts in preaching or exhortation, we note an incongruity: There are two totally different approaches to the "book." One seeks in it irrefutable "truths"; the other seeks an inspiration, a power, a guide for life and action, an answer to anguish or an expression of happiness. One tries to lean on the "letter" without any doubt and to interpret it from the positivism of "common sense"; the other discerns in it what "the Spirit says" and interprets it in the realm of "miracle." These are two ways of "living out the Bible"; for fundamentalism it is "objective testimony," in some way "external," which "is there." The Pentecostal, as Campos says, "feels part of the text, 'retells the Bible,' feels 'congenial with the text,'" and thus can actualize it, relive it in his or her situation, prolong it. In theological tradition this has been called "spiritual interpretation," and it has taken various forms and occupied an important place in the life of the church.

One might well say that these "two ways of living out the Bible" can coexist — in reality they do — and even be compatible. I believe things are more complex. On one hand, the conception of Scripture and the cultural tradition that operate in fundamentalism carry implicit theological and ideological visions that limit the conceptual horizon of Pentecostalism. The fact that its freedom for a "spiritual" interpretation takes place "despite" the fundamentalist conception impedes that Scripture function adequately as a "control" on the freedom of interpretation. Instead of being a "mediation" that allows fluid communication and a healthy interrelation between text and experience, the fundamentalist conception "interrupts" that relationship in both directions; neither can the dynamic of Pentecostal personal and social experience adequately inform the reading of the text, nor can the text provide a dynamic and constructive critique of the former. To be sure, the work of the Spirit often surpasses these contradictions. But how much richer the experience, the practice, and the reading would be without the drag of a hermeneutical scheme that has little to do with the true identity of the experience and the faith of the believer!

Insofar as this criticism is justified, the Pentecostal theologian is called to rethink, from within his/her community, the hermeneutical categories that correspond both to the way in which the community "lives the Scripture" and to the necessary "respect" for the distance the text holds even within the unity text/experience and text/practice.

Without slighting the contributions of biblical studies and the history of interpretation to influence this reflection, following are what I would call three fundamental dimensions of the experience of the Bible in Pentecostalism that would be the "ingredients" which a Pentecostal "hermeneutics" would include in this reflection. First, the Bible as a *story* that is heard, repeated, and memorized in worship, study, and in daily reading — as against the Bible as a repository of proof texts. Then, the Bible as the *instrument* by which the Spirit guides us in the midst of all kinds of alternatives and decisions that we have to resolve. Finally, the Bible as a *"language"* which is expressive of the living of the faith — fear, joy, praise, confession, supplication.

2. "For salvation is nearer to us now than when we became believers" (Rom. 13:11). Sepúlveda explains for us the significance of the hope of the "near return" of the Lord in the experience of the "excluded." He also has indicated that Pentecostals can no longer see themselves simply as "excluded." In truth, they are at both shores of the growing sea of exclusion — among whom, precariously, they have set foot on solid land and try there to assure their abiding place, and also among many others who struggle without success to emerge from the waters. In both cases, the need to find "a place in the world" is for them essential, and they try to open a way to satisfy it. Some cling to a "gospel of prosperity" that promises them security, material progress, and tranquillity as an almost automatic consequence of faith.

Others try to help themselves and others by means of different forms of social solidarity. Some aspire to join the building of the worldly city through social and political participation. In none of these cases do they find that the premillennial, and sometimes dispensationalist, apocalypticism they have received responds to their living situation and their historical experience. The result, I believe, is that the apocalyptic view — the fourth pillar of classic theology: "the Lord returns" — transforms itself into a rather empty affirmation, or tends to be left aside.

This loss would be lamentable. The apocalyptic dimension is, in effect, a constitutive part of evangelical faith, inseparable from the New Testament message, and is needed to give meaning to, and define the character of, a responsible participation in history. That must be, however, purified from some of the features acquired in the millennial and escapist Anglo-Saxon fundamentalism of the end of the last century[33] and returned to its biblical meaning: the affirmation of God's power in the midst of the nonpower of those who have been sacrificed on earth; the call to "resistance" (upomone) against the enslaving powers of this world and the announcement of the final triumph of the crucified King; judgment upon the agents of iniquity; and an end to the sway of injustice, cruelty, oppression, destruction, and death, not as a mere "escape" for the individual soul to another world but as the coming of the kingdom of God as the destiny of history and of the world. In this perspective, the community of the resurrected Messiah becomes a place where the Holy Spirit builds a "sign" of the new world and believers are witnesses to that new reality which we await.[34]

---

33. On the importance of millennialism as a central element of fundamentalism there has been an interesting debate between Ernest Sandeen, *The Roots of Fundamentalism: British and American Millenarianism, 1800-1930* (Chicago: University of Chicago Press, 1970), and George Marsden, "Defining Fundamentalism," in *Christian Scholar's Review* 1 (1971): 141-51, and Sandeen's reply in the following number of the same publication. While Sandeen considers millennialism the "root" of fundamentalism, Marsden sees it as "one of the roots" of a movement whose definitive characteristic is the rejection of modernity.

34. In his book on Pentecostal spirituality, Steven Land has interpreted "Pentecostal spirituality as apocalyptic vision," interpreting the experience of the Spirit as both anticipation and first fruits of the kingdom and "participation [in celebration and community life] in the story of God" that moves toward the glorious consummation. Steven J. Land, *Pentecostal Spirituality: A Passion for the Kingdom* (Sheffield: Sheffield Academic Press, 1994), esp. chap. 2.

This reconceptualization of language and of biblical symbols about the "end" and the relationship of the end to history and to the church cannot be simply the result of a theological revision; it has to be the theological and biblical accompaniment of the experience of faith, struggle, and suffering itself, but also of power and hope for believers.[35]

I make these observations with a keen awareness that they are very tentative. I would hope they would be seen only as open questions. I cannot pretend, from my own experience and training, to formulate a response that has to be given in the Pentecostal's life, experience, and reflection itself. I intend, quite simply, to submit these questions to my Pentecostal brothers and sisters, as a sign of respect and fellowship, in the freedom of the evangelical faith we share.

35. An important discussion of the contemporary relevance of the "apocalyptic gospel of Paul," and at the same time a sharp critique of the deformations and adulterations it has undergone, is found in J. Christian Beker, *Paul's Apocalyptic Gospel: The Coming Triumph of God* (Philadelphia: Fortress, 1989).

4. An Ethnic Face of Protestantism?

IN THE PROLOGUE to his notable and pioneer work on Brazilian Protestantism, Emile Léonard indicates that "we omit consideration of the foreign colony churches, *whose problems, that do not present anything specifically Brazilian,* will not be discussed here."[1] It is curious that as perspicacious an author as Léonard — who states that his purpose was to study "the institutional and practical problems posed by the planting and development of beliefs and churches" and "of the 'social corpus' in which these beliefs are incarnate, creating realities in the churches, human realities, with all their peculiarities" — would not find anything specifically Brazilian in the planting and development of the numerous Protestant communities — mainly German, but also Japanese, Lithuanian, Dutch — that arrived very early in Brazil.

Indeed, their very arrival, as was that of a substantial part of the "immigration Protestantism," was not fortuitous nor without meaning. As we indicated with reference to the mission churches, in agreement with Bastian, one must repeat that these immigrants did not arrive as a natural phenomenon by their own impetus, but rather in response to general immigration policies, if not express invitations, of the same modernizing elites that opened the doors to the missions. This very fact defined in large measure, from the outset, the locations chosen, the material conditions, the status given them, the difficulties encountered, and hence the ideological, institutional, and theological responses that

1. Emile-G. Léonard, *O Protestantismo Brasileiro: Estudo de Eclesiologia e de Historia Social* (Sao Paulo: ASTE, 1964), p. 17, emphasis mine.

developed. In this sense, despite their great differences, there was one common denominator: the moment and historical conditions in which the "mission" churches and "immigration" churches entered Latin America. This common moment included the place they occupied in the conscience and purpose of Latin American leaders, and the social, cultural, and religious conditions that they had to face. That the two types of churches responded in different ways to these conditions is precisely one of the subjects that merit study, for it can tell us something about the character of each.[2]

I. How to Approach This Problem?

A. A Language Problem Which Goes beyond Language

These churches were given diverse designations: Daniel P. Monti (referring to the River Plate, 1967) and Bastian speak of "residents' churches" (meaning resident "foreigners"), but it was far more common to speak of "immigration churches." This is the designation adopted by Damboriena, Deiros, and Prien *(Einwanderungsprotestantismus)*. Research on these churches in Argentina, carried out by a team of the Center for Christian Studies, directed by Christian Lalive d'Epinay, appears under the title *The Transplanted Churches*.[3] Each of these expressions "say something" about these religious communities. The first two point to their way of entry; the third suggests the manner. Both are, nonetheless, insufficient and could turn out to be equivocal. To speak of these churches as "residents" or "immigrant" seems to suggest that what would characterize these churches is their *external* origin — they came "from outside." This is true, however, of all the churches that entered Latin America, including the Roman Catholic Church. This is not just a truism; "coming from outside" means that they arrived from the context of a culture, language, institutional structures, mores, and customs molded in another place and another time. The image of "transplanta-

2. We do not deem it necessary to try to summarize the historical data on the entrance of immigration churches to Latin America. The works of Prien, Bastian, Deiros, and others to which we have referred provide the basic data and include the necessary bibliographical references to take up a more detailed historical study.

3. Waldo L. Villalpando, ed., *Las Iglesias del Trasplante: Protestantismo de Inmigración en la Argentina* (Buenos Aires: CEC, 1970).

tion," as Villalpando indicates in his prologue, was taken from one of my writings in which I quote the conclusion to which Robert Ricard arrived in a study of the planting of the Catholic church in Mexico: "what was established in Mexico," says Ricard, "was not a Mexican church but a Spanish church transplanted to Mexico."[4] *Mutatis mutandis,* Villalpando would note, that is what occurred with the immigration churches in Argentina. The analogy, however, is not totally exact: the Spanish Catholic church was brought to America *and imposed on an autochthonous population;* the immigration churches were brought *with the original population in which they were born.*

In truth, pressing matters a bit, we could say that it is the very nature of Christian faith, due to its inevitable historical reference, to be "transported" by witnesses from one place — let us say, Palestine — and "introduced" in another place. It cannot be born "spontaneously" from a culture or a preexistent religiosity. What does make a difference are the "modes" of "immigration." These also differ considerably among the various immigration Protestant churches in our situation: Some are peasant "colonies" — Welsh in Argentina or Mennonite in Paraguay; others are commercial implants — rural estate owners or managers in the provinces of Buenos Aires or Patagonia or employees of British firms in Chile or Argentina; others still are "colored" laborers imported for public works — railroads or plantations in Central America or Brazil. They also vary in the ways of transplantation: In some cases it was direct and structurally the creation of an official "subsidiary," an extension of national churches in the country of origin; in others it was the immigration of groups of the same national and religious origin who gathered and organized themselves in their new location in the country to which they had immigrated. Another still was the situation in recent years of immigrations from Oriental nations — Korea, Japan, Taiwan — linked to mission denominations in their own countries of origin where they were also minorities. Much could be said about these differentiations, but the question is: Is there something in common more meaningful and profound than their external origin?

4. Robert Ricard, *La conquete spirituelle du Mexique* (Paris, 1933); ET, *The Spiritual Conquest of Mexico: An Essay on the Apostolate and the Evangelizing Methods of Mendicant Orders in New Spain, 1523-1572* (Berkeley: University of California Press, 1966), cited in J. Míguez, "Las perspectivas del cristianismo en América Latina," *Cuadernos de Embalse,* FUMEC, 1964, pp. 1-13.

B. Ethnic Churches?

I believe that it is in the attempt to answer the aforementioned question that the phrase "ethnic churches" has begun to be used. Here one is not just speaking about origin or mode of entry but rather of the very nature of a church, not of a historical accident but of a constitutive characteristic. As we shall see, this broad designation complicates the matter, but it also opens up a more profound and significant theological theme than merely the mention of origin or mode of entry.

It is complicated, first, because it widens the panorama. If, in very basic terms, the distinctive characteristic of these churches is their "ethnic homogeneity," then indigenous churches enter the picture, such as the Toba United Church in Argentina or the Miskito Moravian indigenous churches in Nicaragua, or almost exclusively black churches in Panama, to mention only a few.

It is complicated also, and more importantly, because it introduces the complex and debated category of what is ethnic. Anthropological studies have debated, and continue to debate, an adequate definition or identification of what an "ethnic group" is and what is "ethnicity." In 1964, in a frequently quoted article, Raoul Naroll pointed to four common indicators used by anthropologists to define an "ethnic group"; Fredrik Barth summarizes Naroll in these terms:

> The term ethnic group is generally understood in anthropological literature . . . to designate a population which: (a) is largely biologically self-perpetuating; (b) shares fundamental cultural values, realized in overt unity in cultural forms; (c) makes up a field of communication and interaction; (d) has a membership which identifies itself, and is identified by others, as constituting a category distinguishable from other categories of the same order.[5]

Last century, an anthropology largely oriented toward the study of so-called primitive cultures placed emphasis on objective factors such as biological self-reproduction and cultural mores. Later, a growing con-

---

5. *Process and Form in Social Life: Selected Essays of Fredrik Barth* (London and Boston: Routledge and Kegan Paul, 1970), 1:199f. Barth refers to an article by Raoul Naroll, "On Ethnic Unit Classification," published in *Current Anthropology* 5, no. 4 (1964): 283-312, followed by a very interesting discussion by well-known anthropologists and Naroll's own response. This whole issue merits a careful study.

sciousness in social sciences of subjective values as well as of the mobility of migrations which constantly create new ethnic minorities led to under-lining the importance of communication and interaction in the social webs created by self-ascription — those who identify themselves con-sciously with a community or group — and ascription by others — those who are identified by others as belonging to that group. On the other hand, the importance of transformation processes that take place within ethnic groups has also been pointed out. It is no longer possible to maintain a static view, as if ethnic cultures reproduce themselves without modifica-tions across time and space. Finally, it is important to note the plurality of ascriptions which occur in modern society. A person can identify himself or herself as ethnically "German" but also "middle class" socially, "agnos-tic" religiously, and "socialist" ideologically or politically. That is, the dimensions within which an ethnic identity is determined may vary. Also, the communication networks and the organizations established based on ethnic identity can define limits in various ways: for example, admitting or rejecting, on the basis of ideological, political, or religious options, or the use of the same language.[6]

All this should lead us to be very cautious in speaking about "ethnic churches" as if we were defining a homogeneous and static unity, wholly identifiable in terms of national origin, language, and a series of uniform and immutable cultural practices. The importance and significance of the religious dimension in the definition of ethnic identity vary consid-erably from one group to another, and within the same group from one moment to another.[7]

6. We have found some writings that clearly and simply summarize this discussion in the book edited by Fredrik Barth in Spanish, *Los grupos étnicos y sus fronteras* (Mexico: Fondo de Cultura Económica, 1976), pp. 9-49, and in the compilation edited by Roberto Ringuelet, *Procesos de contacto interétnico* (Buenos Aires: Ediciones Búsqueda, 1987), pp. 13-48. Both include abundant bibliographies.

7. In his book *Brésil, terre de contrastes* (Paris: Hachette, 1957), p. 241, Roger Bastide makes a strong statement on the role of religion in cultural preservation, which Villalpando quotes (*Las Iglesias del Trasplante*, p. 9) as a clue for interpreting "trans-planted churches":

Generally, religion is the most important center of resistance. Language, ways of living, and ideas about love can be changed. Religion integrates the last trench around which crystalize those values that do not want to die. The holy *(le sacre)* is, in the battles between civilizations, the last bulwark that will not surrender.

In some of the "ethnic awakenings" which — to the surprise of many — have growing

In the following section we shall try to illustrate some of these variations as we consider the characteristics of "ethnic churches," mainly in churches which originated by immigration in the Southern Cone of South America.[8]

II. Mission Protestantism and Ethnic Protestantism

The distance and lack of communication between mission churches and ethnic churches, at least until almost fifty years ago, is an undeniable fact. Even more, we could speak of a lack of confidence and a mutual unwillingness to accept the legitimacy of the other. Not one of the churches resulting from immigration — already present for half a century in Argentina, Uruguay, and Brazil (to refer only to that part of the Southern Cone) — participated in the 1916 Panama Congress. In Montevideo, in 1925, there was a representative of the Waldensian church, one of the French Protestant Committee, and one of the Scots Presbyterian Church — all of Reformed origin — in addition to the Lutheran church which at that point had become a mission church. However, there was no representation of the immigration churches in the Protestant Congress in Havana

---

strength in various parts of the world, this statement of Bastide's would seem to be confirmed. I think, however, that as a generalization it should be taken with caution. It is true that among these "ethnic awakenings" are some in which religion plays an important role (if only ideologically), but other factors such as language, political or ideological commitments, and common economic interests play at least the same important role in self-affirmation and in ethnic struggles.

8. Given the impossibility, as much for reasons of space as of knowledge, to consider this topic on the basis of primary sources, and in relation to the great diversity of presumably ethnic churches in Latin America, I have decided to offer only some observations based on research studies about some churches in the Southern Cone, particularly Argentina, Uruguay, and Brazil. With reference to Brazil I have mainly used, along with the historical work of Mendonça, cited earlier, the books of Martin N. Dreher, *Igreja e Germanidade: Estudo crítico da historia da Igreja Evangelica de Confissao Luterana no Brasil* (Caxias do Sul, RS: Editora Sinodal/Editora da Universidade de Caxias do Sul, 1984); André Droogers, *Religiosidade Popular Luterana, Relatório sobre una pesquisa no Espírito Santo en Julho 1982* (Sao Leopoldo: Editora Sinodal, 1984); and Hans-Jürgen Prien, *Evangelische Kirchenwerdung in Brasilien* (Gutersloh: Guthersloher Verlagshaus Gerd Molin, 1989). In Argentina, the mentioned *Las Iglesias del Trasplante* and the thesis of Maria M. Berg, "Dinamarca bajo la cruz del sur: los asentamientos daneses del centro-sur de la provincia de Buenos Aires, 1850-1930" (Universidad de Buenos Aires, 1994). Other indications appear in the various references.

in 1929. It was only at the First Latin American Protestant Conference (Buenos Aires, 1949) that the Waldensian church, the French Speaking Protestant Church, the Mennonite Churches of Paraguay, and (as an observer) the German Evangelical Synod of the River Plate were present. The Confederation of Protestant Churches of the River Plate (Argentina and Uruguay), created in 1939, already had four "ethnic" churches, and three others joined in the 1940-49 period.[9]

A. Rejection and Mutual Lack of Recognition

Mutual stereotypes can easily be detected. The ethnic churches looked, in the eyes of the mission churches, like *state churches, inclined to Catholicism, formal and "worldly."* Frequently there were references that identified them as the European Protestantism and Anglicanism, which led to the decision of the 1910 Edinburgh Missionary Conference to exclude Latin America since it was "a Christian continent" and therefore not a "mission field." Liturgical order, the use of a foreign language, and the unwillingness to engage in "proselytism" were incomprehensible and scandalous to the missionary and evangelizing mentality of the "evangelicals." In addition, using alcoholic beverages or tobacco, dancing, and other social activities of some of these churches clashed with the Puritan ethic of the majority of the mission churches.

Concomitantly, the immigration churches brought from their roots a strong suspicion regarding the "free churches," which often were seen in their countries of origin as practicing proselytism in detriment of the regional "peoples' churches" *(Volkskirche).* Their piety appeared disorderly, fanatic, or "enthusiastic," appropriate to "sects" which, still in the well-known German *vade mecum* of Kurt Hutten (third ed., 1954), were typified as "Seher, Grübler, Enthusiasten" (visionaries, vain, fanatic).[10] Besides, the

9. This data is documented, respectively, by the reports of the Panama, Montevideo, and Havana Congresses cited in prior chapters. With regard to the Confederación Evangélica del Río de la Plata, see Horacio Gualdieri, *FAIE: Apuntes para una historia de las relaciones eclesiasles en el Río de la Plata* (Buenos Aires, n.d., mimeographed), and Eugenio E. Mohr, "Confederación de Iglesias Evangélicas del Río de la Plata," thesis presented to ISEDET, Buenos Aires, 1993.

10. Kurt Hutten, *Seher, Grübler, Enthusiasten: Sekten und religiose Sondergemeindschaften der Gegenwart,* 3rd ed. (Stuttgart: Quell Verlag, 1954). In the early editions until at least 1954, churches such as the Methodist, Nazarene, etc., appear under the desig-

fiery and repetitive preaching sounded to them superficial, lacking a solid confessional or doctrinal base.

Of course, there always were exceptions at the personal level, particularly among some foreign missionaries in the mission churches whose ecumenical relations had put them in touch with European churches and national leaders who had a wider training and experience. Also there were exceptions at the institutional level, especially between the Waldensian and Methodist churches, which cooperated in theological education (save for some brief intervals) from the decade of the 1880s on (including the Disciples of Christ from 1917 on).

It was toward the close of the 1930 decade, however, that cordial relationships and cooperation began to develop between the immigration churches and those of mission identified with what we have called the "liberal face" of Latin American Protestantism, in the framework of the previously mentioned Confederation of Protestant Churches of the River Plate (1939), and subsequently of Argentina and Uruguay, of the Literature Committee of CCLA (Committee on Cooperation in Latin America, 1925), and of theological education in the associations of theological study institutions (Asociación Sudamericana de Instituciones Teológicas [ASIT] in the southern region, and others in Brazil, the Caribbean, and the northern region), which were organized from 1960 on. Not all suspicions have vanished. When in the 1950 decade there was the possibility that the Argentine Reformed Church (of Dutch Reformed origin) might enter the ecumenical association which at that time sponsored the Protestant Union Theological Seminary in Buenos Aires, even though there were already Calvinist "associate members" (the Board of Missions of the northern Presbyterian Church in the U.S.A. and the Waldensian church itself), several questions were raised — which at times seemed theological, such as presumed Calvinist fundamentalism. Other questions had to do with ethnic modalities, and still others with an instinctive lack of confidence toward an "ethnic" European church, and entry had to wait until 1970, when the Instituto Superior Evangélico de Estudios Teologicos (ISEDET) was organized with a wider presence of "immigration churches."[11]

---

nation of "perfectionist communities." In the eighth edition of 1962 the Methodists disappear but the Nazarenes continue under the same rubric.

11. I make this observation on the basis of indirect references and of comments involved in these conversations, but I do not know of specific documentation on the subject.

Readers who consider this panorama from the viewpoint of other areas — the Caribbean, the Pacific countries, Central America, Mexico — will discover parallels and differences, both in time and in modalities, but I dare to believe that the experience of the River Plate region which I have described is not qualitatively different from others. In addition, one must point out that, from the 1949 Protestant Conference on, there has continued at the Latin American level a relationship, whose institutional embodiment has been the Comisión pro Unidad Evangélica Latinoamericana (UNELAM) and later CLAI, which has developed very widely and in which there has been an equal leading participation of mission and ethnic churches. The same was true in movements such as Church and Society in Latin America, the Christian Students Federation and the Student Christian Movements (MECs), and other ecumenical organizations from 1960 onward. It must be indicated, however, that in these Latin American Protestant organisms — and in many of the related local bodies as well — the participation and support of the streams we have called evangelical and Pentecostal were at best partial and tentative. In fact, alternative unity structures have emerged (such as CONELA or the congresses of CLADE I and CLADE II) with which relationships have been established only recently, as indicated in a prior chapter.

B. Where Are the Frontiers?

These rather anecdotal observations pose, nevertheless, a more fundamental question that needs to be addressed if the misunderstandings are truly to be surpassed and a fruitful and lasting relation be established: that is, where do the *true* frontiers run? What really separates these currents of Latin American Protestantism? This question cannot be answered unilaterally from any one of these currents, nor superficially in the service of goodwill and an open attitude, even if these are essential. Happily, I believe we have at hand optimal conditions to discuss this topic. I also believe that we have started on this route in the area of ecumenical practice, in ministerial training, in witness and in common effort in matters of social order, in the defense of human rights, and in the distribution of the Scriptures. Still, we owe ourselves and we owe the Lord at least two tasks. One is to incorporate effectively into this relationship the evangelical and Pentecostal currents of missional Protestantism — and that cannot mean the "absorption" of the others in ecumenical structures and relationships we already have, but rather their revision or modification, or even going beyond them to re-create *together* the structures and relationships that will effectively take up the legitimate and serious questions presented to us by those currents. The other is to consider in depth the theme of "mission and evangelization" and "ethnic identity" that may be the central issues, or perhaps *the* central theological and ecclesial question raised by this relationship. Meanwhile, and as a humble contribution to this task, I should like to explore some stretches of this "frontier" and see if it is only an imaginary or artificial line, or if it truly exists, and where the milestones are that mark the trace of its course.

1. *A first line of demarcation would be that which, using the vocabulary current in European Protestant churches, runs between the "free churches" and the "territorial" or "national" or "peoples" churches* (Volkskirchen), linked some way organically to the state, or at least to the nation. The classic work of Ernst Troeltsch in 1912, *Die Soziallehren der christlichen Kirchen und Gruppen* (The social doctrines of Christian churches and groups),[12] established the use of the terms "church" and "sect" as characteristic sociological categories. *Churches* conceive themselves as coterminous with a people, integrated into the national culture and frequently organically related to the state. People belong to these churches by birth and therefore do not engage in proselytism beyond their frontiers. *Sects,* in contrast, are voluntary groupings, often of minorities, into which one enters by personal decision. They practice "believer's baptism," are countercultural, do not maintain any ties to the state, and do practice proselytism.[13] Unfortunately, Troeltsch's and Max Weber's vocabulary became loaded with meanings that the authors did not intend, transforming a sociological description into a struggle for doctrinal, even legal, legitima-

12. Ernst Troeltsch, *Die Soziallehren der christlichen Kirchen und Gruppen,* in *Gesammelte Schriften,* 3d ed. (Tubingen: J. C. B. Mohr, 1923), 1:331-49, 691-94; ET, *The Social Teaching of the Christian Churches* (Louisville: Westminster/John Knox, 1992), 1:358-77, 794-97.

13. In addition to the work of Troeltsch cited in the previous note, see Max Weber, "Die protestantische Sekten," in *Gesammelte Aufsatze zur Religionssoziologie,* 1:207-36. The distinctions of Troeltsch and Weber have subsequently been refined, including more precise and specific categories as: universal church, ecclesia, established sect, and sect. See in this respect J. Milton Yinger, *Religion, Society, and the Individual: An Introduction to the Sociology of Religion* (New York: Macmillan, 1957), pp. 142-55.

tion. What is at stake, indeed, are "two forms of being the church" which have run side by side throughout history, at least since the fourth century, and whose theological basis and missionary and pastoral conceptions will surely continue, not necessarily between particular churches but in the very heart of those same churches. Nevertheless, I believe — at least in the Latin American situation — that we must relativize the differences between these two models.

On the one hand, the very concept of a relationship between church and people/nation/ethnic group varies in different "ethnic" churches. Anglicanism, for example, seems to think of itself as the religious dimension of the nation and deems that in each nation an autonomous national church should be organized. For that reason it was originally proposed to create a church on the Anglican model in the newly independent United States of America, not as an extension of the Anglican Church of England but as an autonomous church. Such a relationship to the state was impossible in the religious panorama of the United States, and the Episcopal Church was, in reality, one of the "free churches" in the pluralistic religious field of the country.[14] In Latin America, Anglicanism faced a dilemma: Either it recognized the Roman Catholic Church as "the church" of the Latin American nation — which it in fact did in many cases — and hence reduced its activity to minister to the "English expatriates" and their descendants as a kind of "chaplaincy" to the English nation on foreign soil, or to evangelize the "autochthonous indigenous nations" not reached by the Catholic church, as was also done by the missionary societies of the Church of England. Or it became a "free church," *one* of the churches that "compete" in the Latin American religious arena. This seems to be the option taken by the Episcopal Church, as Kater defines it in a study of the Central American region:

14. In a reflection on Anglicanism in "the Central Region of America," the education officer of the Panama Episcopal Church, John L. Kater, describes this Anglican concept, citing the classic formulation of Hooker, "each Church was originally organized to minister to a people or a particular nation. . . . The imposition of the Papal monarchy . . . was a late development, which stripped the churches of their ability to minister adequately to their own nation." Then Kater shows how that concept could not function in the United States and ended in a theory of "different branches" of the church and hence pluralism. In Ashton J. Brooks, ed., *Eclesiología: presencia anglicana en la Región Central de América* (San José, Costa Rica: DEI, 1990).

Once again, Anglican identity and the ecclesial models that have defined Anglicanism are at stake. Latin American Anglicanism can play an active role in the reflection process, so that together, and in dialogue with Christians of other traditions, we Anglicans can seek other *church models* that better fit reality in this continent, and that of others.[15]

Some of the "ethnic" churches entered or consolidated themselves in Latin America at moments when their nations of origin achieved national unity. Thus it was in Germany, unified under Bismarck in 1871. To a different degree, it was also the case with Danish migration to Argentina, the bulk of which came after 1875 when "new nationalist breezes began to blow from the south of Jutland after the war of 1864."[16] It was logical that the identification of church and nationhood would express itself with greater force in such situations, even though, as we shall see, in a somewhat different form in each of these cases.[17] In Brazil, as well as in Uruguay and Argentina, this linkage of nationality and church profoundly marked the life of the churches of German origin, creating deep tensions, including divisions.[18]

We mention, thirdly, churches that, though ethnically homogeneous and similar to the former in some of the traits arising from this situation, lived out a different relationship with nationhood. Such was the case in the Waldensian church, historically a minority church,

15. Ibid., p. 33.

16. Berg, p. 277.

17. Though, for reasons we shall mention, that is not the case of the Italian Protestant (Waldensian) immigration, it is interesting to note that the Italian colony in Argentina felt strongly the pressure of the consolidation of Italian unity for an "Italian national identity" in place of the identities of regional origin which had prevailed formerly. Cf. Eduardo J. Míguez, "Tensiones de identidad. Reflexiones sobre la experiencia italiana inmigrante en la Argentina," in *Asociacionismo, trabajo e identidad étnica: Los italianos en América Latina en una perspectiva comparada*, ed. F. J. Devoto and E. J. Míguez (Buenos Aires: CEMLA-CSER-IEHS, 1992), pp. 333-58.

18. We shall not stop to consider the complex problem of ethnic "German" identity and the "German" nation which, as we indicate further on, manifests itself in some later schisms, nor shall we consider the debated question of support or opposition to the "Germanism" urged by national socialism. This subject is discussed, with reference to Brazil, in the writings of Dreher and Prien already mentioned. With regard to Argentina and Uruguay, there is a very illuminating article of Alejandro Zorzín (part of research he pursues), "Pastor Wilhelm Nelke, un impulsor de la *germanidad* en el Río de la Plata," in *Cuadernos de Teología* 12, no. 2, 1992 (Buenos Aires: ISEDET): 29-57.

persecuted for a long time in its nation of origin, for which the religious tradition, the "patois" language, and the identification with the "Waldensian valley" of the Piedmont were stronger than the ties to national identity, though ideologically it may have coincided with the liberal and anticlerical stream represented by Garibaldi which achieved the unity.[19] Such was also the case of Dutch immigration, identified principally with the Reformed Churches of Holland which, after the 1834 schism, consolidated in 1869 to form the *Christelijke Gereformeerde Kerken in Nederland* and remained separated from the Dutch Reformed Church, which was more closely tied to the state.

In addition, one must note that, though the "ethnic" churches were often "state churches" in their countries of origin, they were in some instances liberated to become in fact "free churches," or were forced to do so by the very nature of the situation. For example, German immigration came to Brazil from 1823/24 on, considerably earlier than German unification. With reference to these early migrations, Walter Altmann makes an interesting observation: "Among aspects that turned out to be most pleasing [to these early immigrants] were, without doubt, the possibility of *organizing their religious communities autonomously*. Free communities were established, free of the tutelage of ecclesiastical bodies dominated, as state churches, by the territorial German governments."[20] Moreover, they had frequently to pay their pastors' salaries and to maintain their congregations economically when support from abroad was insufficient or was interrupted, and that contributed to a sense of autonomy. More important, they were faced by a "national church," a *Volkskirche* — the Roman Catholic Church — which enjoyed in exclusivity the relationships with the society that had molded their own "status" and characteristics in their countries of origin. Now they

19. In his *Storia dei Valdesi* (Torino: Editrice Claudiana, 1980), 3:96, Valdo Vinay makes this interesting observation: "In their innermost being the Protestants [*evangelisti* in the original] rejoiced at national independence. . . . But the spirituality of the awakening [*risvegliata*] rigorously separated the spiritual and political spheres, and they could not see an effective vital link between the gospel preached and the political and social liberation of their people." Cf. also Giorgio Tourn, *Los Valdenses*, vol. 3, bk. 2 (Montevideo: Edición Iglesia Valdense, 1983), pp. 274ff.; ET, *The Waldensians: The First 800 Years (1174-1974)* (Torino: Claudiana; New York, 1980, distributed in North America by the American Waldensian Aid Society).

20. Walter Altmann, *Confrontación y Liberación: una perspectiva Latinoamericana sobre Martín Lutero* (Buenos Aires: ISEDET, 1987), p. 83, emphasis mine.

had to operate, not as "peoples' churches" but as churches of a limited social, cultural, and religious "space," often threatened or discriminated against.[21]

While we must take account of all these qualifications, I think we should recognize that there is a difference in the mode in which certain churches that we call mission churches and others usually designated as immigration churches placed themselves in society. In my opinion, the difference resides in that the former prolonged and reproduced in Latin America, under different religious conditions but in an anthropologically and in part politically analogous situation, the North American experience of the nineteenth century. The Methodist theologian Albert Outler has characterized this experience as an "immense and complex upwelling of the Spirit that rescued the Christian cause and defined [North American] Protestantism for the better part of a century."

> It turned revivalism from an episodic affair to a permanent institution. It relegated the sacraments and Christian nurture to a marginal role and its own theological ethos came to be identified as the distinctive meaning of the word "evangelical" in America. . . .
>
> The most obvious feature of the Second Awakening was its emotional fervor — always focused on two points, and almost only these two: (1) salvation — deliverance from sin and guilt (hellfire and damnation) and (2) a self-inhibitory morality. . . .
>
> The Second Great Awakening represented the effective triumph in the New World of that "radical Protestantism" that had been so sternly suppressed in Europe by the dominant Lutheran, Reformed and Anglican state-churches. This Protestant tradition was largely "Montanist" in its ecclesiology (low church, free-church), anti-sacerdotal, anti-sacramental, anti-intellectualist. It made a pejorative distinction between speculative theology and existential faith. It was suspicious of a learned clergy. It regarded conversion as more typically the climax

---

21. It is worth noting here that, even though having been welcomed and even invited, foreign communities were often discriminated against socially, rejected by traditional elites, and frequently suffered the political vicissitudes of the various countries. In the exercise of their religion, they experienced serious problems in matters such as the construction of churches, marriage and burial of their members, and the religious education of their children, and they had serious conflicts with the state which often were only overcome by the intervention of diplomatic representatives of the countries of origin.

of Christian experience than its initiation. It insisted on personal religion as the only real essence of Christianity.[22]

As we have indicated, neither do all the mission churches fit this scheme, nor are all the immigration churches alien to it. I believe, however, that there is a certain truth in this picture, and that it can help us understand ourselves better within the total Latin American evangelical-Protestant family.

2. These considerations go beyond the sociological and political area and lead us to a second line of demarcation worth exploring: that which refers to the theology of these two types of churches. In principle, it might seem simple to confront "Reformation churches" that have a classical Lutheran or Calvinist doctrine with mission churches that developed out of Anglo-Saxon dissident churches. Samuel Escobar has made this distinction, drawing — much as Outler did — on the ecclesial and theological heritage of Latin American evangelical Protestantism from "the radical Reformation" of the sixteenth century — "voluntary" churches, free of state tutelage, critical of the dominant culture, and often socially tied to poor or marginalized sectors.[23] With reference to the United States, Richard Niebuhr offered a similar interpretation in his classic work, *The Social Sources of Denominationalism.*[24]

Undoubtedly there is here a difference to keep in mind. If, for example, we take the work of Lalive d'Epinay regarding ten immigration churches in Argentina,[25] we discover some significant indications: All

---

22. Albert C. Outler, *Evangelism in the Wesleyan Spirit* (Nashville: Tidings, 1971), pp. 60-61, emphasis mine.

23. Samuel Escobar, *La fe evangélica y las teologías de la liberación* (El Paso, Tex.: Baptist Publishing House, 1987), p. 45ff.

24. H. Richard Niebuhr, *The Social Sources of Denominationalism* (New York: Meridian Books, 1957; original edition 1929). Niebuhr sees, throughout history, the emergence of the "churches of the disinherited" as a protest against the "accommodation" of the churches to the interests of the dominant classes and to their inability to maintain an ethical and prophetic witness to Christian faith. With reference to the Reformation and the radical movements of the sixteenth century, see pp. 34-53, and a general thesis on the social origin of denominationalism, pp. 21-25.

25. The study documented in the book is limited to ten churches. In his concluding summaries, Lalive d'Epinay adds the French Speaking Protestant Church of the River Plate, whose data he knows but does not include (Villalpando, ed., p. 164, n. 6). I have not considered that fact and have limited myself to the data in the book; hence the difference between my data and his figures.

of them consider "order in worship and in spiritual life" among the three guidelines "which that denomination especially emphasizes"; some of them place that in first place, one places the Eucharist in first place, one justification by faith, and one conversion and the new birth. Of course the result would have been different in evangelical or Pentecostal churches. Lalive d'Epinay himself points to a marked difference in "the type of piety":

> It is interesting to note that the items which define an "ardent" *(hot)* spirituality . . . never were mentioned while ten denominations insisted on *order,* on a "cool" piety life (cool, if we are allowed to use these catch words of pietism but also of jazz language). Here there is a consensus regarding the *style* of religious life, and also a certain rationalism of faith (healing would be a concept of medicine rather than of religious life).[26]

Another interesting observation, also highlighted by Lalive d'Epinay, is that eight of the ten churches choose, as to the authority of the Bible, an alternative that recognizes it as "inspired in its 'essence' and ideas, but the writers, as human beings, may have introduced errors (outdated concepts)."[27] This reply would probably also be common in the "liberal" churches, but not in evangelical and Pentecostal ones.

The survey is significant, but it requires some comments. (a) It is a quantitative survey whose technique is a "spread of responses" (multiple choice), that is, the formulation of possible answers is determined by the surveyor. (b) It involves a survey of church "leaders" — mainly pastors. I have the impression, after many years of experience with churches, that a qualitative investigation that includes various membership levels could significantly alter the replies — probably with more "evangelical" replies in the immigration churches. (c) More important, the alternatives set forth in the "doctrinal" section of the survey seem to me aimed at indicating items where the possibility of discrepancies is most likely — glossolalia and prophecy, healing, committed participation in society (indicated by memberships in clubs, unions, or political parties) — rather than exploring the truly prevailing theologies in the piety and teaching of those churches.

I am not trying to ignore or minimize the differences this survey

26. Ibid., p. 165.
27. Ibid., p. 164.

shows nor to discard its valid observations, such as those mentioned by Escobar, but I should want to place them within a wider historical and religious context. At the historical level one should note that, if "classical" Protestantism was reshaped by its Anglo-Saxon history, which the mission churches received, the history of the immigration churches came from central Europe, which in turn passed through various mediations, sometimes diverse, sometimes concurring. Luther and Calvin, to say it graphically, arrived from Europe after stopping at the ports of Protestant orthodoxy, rationalism, and pietistic movements almost contemporaneously with liberal revisions. Pastors of German, Swiss, French, or Scottish origin, who responded to Lalive d'Epinay in 1970 regarding the authority of Scripture, certainly had read in their seminaries the works of Schlatter or Vinet, Harnack or Hermann, Nygren and Barth. I ask myself, therefore, if a careful study might not indicate that the majority of the pastors of the early migrations would rather represent theological orthodoxy or pietism or liberalism or some mixture of all these in varying proportions. We know of the weight the nineteenth-century awakening had in Scotland and Wales, and also that the influence of these movements was not absent in the Waldensian *risveglio* — awakening — almost at the very moment they set sail for Uruguay and Argentina.[28] In Argentina, both the Argentine Evangelical Lutheran Church (IELA) and the Evangelical Congregational Church, which separated from the (German) Synod of the River Plate, show a strong pietistic and rigorous component. The first was linked to the Missouri Synod in the United States, created under the leadership of C. F. W. Walther, whose adherence to pietism is known, and the second responded in part to an immigration of German groups that lived their

28. This awakening, which came about in the Waldensian churches after the unification (1848), represented various "evangelical" influences — that of reformed pietism, Baptists, Darbyists, Methodists, and evangelical Anglicans, which are well documented in the material earlier mentioned (Vinay, 3:73-165; Tourn, vol. 2, bk. 2, pp. 274ff.). As I was completing this work I came across the recently published work of Roger Geymonat, *El Templo y la Escuela: Los Valdenses en el Uruguay* (Montevideo: Cal y Canto, OBSUR, Fundación Giovanni Agnelli, 1994). Though it does not analyze the theological orientation of the early pastors, one is struck by one aspect that relates to our theme: the contrast between what Geymonat calls "the pietism of the pastors who came from Italy towards the end of the nineteenth century and beginning of the twentieth, filled with a definite spirit of evangelization" and the majority attitude of what "we could describe as the 'passive religious militancy'" of the colonists (pp. 120, 121).

own isolated existence for a long time in Russia — they have been called Russo-Germans or "Volga Germans" — also with a strong pietistic influence (in addition, leaders of the schism related to the U.S. Congregational church). There seem to be in Brazil interesting parallels. On the other hand, in his study of German churches in Brazil, Hans-Jürgen Prien has proven the difficulty of identifying the predominant theological lines of the early pastors. In the only case where there is precise data in the first half of the nineteenth century, that of Pastor Sauerbronn, the theology is what in Germany was called "Neologie," linked to the theologies of Schleiermacher, Nitzch, Neander. Sauerbronn rejected the idea of verbal inspiration and defined "Christian revelation," in the Schleiermacher style, as "rooted" in experience.[29]

These historical references, chosen at random, are not meant to prove that there was theological diversity among the immigration churches, or that within these churches theological stances analogous to those we find in mission churches frequently compete, and often are related to them. My intention is, rather, to point out that these theological differences do not have a major impact on "ethnic" behavior in relation to their surroundings, orthodox or pietistic, biblicist or liberal, "worldly" or "ascetic," coming from state or free churches, *until very recently all tended to understand their mission and the sphere of their responsibility exclusively, or almost exclusively, in terms of the ethnic community.* So much is this true that even churches of strong "evangelical" influence — such as the Congregational and the Argentine Protestant Lutheran churches — that describe themselves as "missionary," define their mission as that of *reactivating the faith of nominal Protestants,* what Lalive d'Epinay calls "internal mission."[30] Even the Evangelical Pentecostal Church (Ukrainian) did not open up to the use of the Spanish language and to evangelization of the local Argentine people until the end of the 1970s.

If these considerations lead us to relativize the difference between mission and immigration churches also in the realm of theology, we must not overlook those differences. I dare to suggest that the tendency of the former is a *pneumatological orientation* and of the latter a *Christological one* in their theologies. I say tendency because neither the one nor the other excludes or relegates Christology or pneumatology. The tendency is seen rather in reference to a more subjective piety in the

29. Prien, pp. 91-93.
30. Lalive d'Epinay, in Villalpando, ed., p. 174.

former and a piety more linked to symbols and objective forms in the latter; to a more face-to-face conception of the church in the one and a more institutional concept in the other; to a more free, circumstantial, and exhortational interpretation of Scripture in the one as against a more exegetical and educational interpretation in the other. It would be very difficult to specify these differences further. Indeed, a more careful and documented study would be needed to justify them. But I do not think I am mistaken in noting that there is a certain "dissonance" that each senses in reference to the "other" communities, along with a sense of "familiarity" in their own communities, that is not just the result of cultural or language differences, but of theological "tone," perceived not so much intellectually as in the manner of feeling and of locating themselves in their religious life.

3. The references in these last paragraphs are conditioned by the fact that some of the ethnic churches at various moments take on a missionary task that goes beyond the ethnic community. I shall here refer — as illustration — to two churches that make this transition under very different circumstances. The United Evangelical Lutheran Church (IELU) has a double origin: In the first (1909-20) the missionaries work with Lutheran immigrants of various languages — Swedish, English, German. From 1920 on, with the arrival of the North American missionary Muller, IELU appears as an evangelizing church among the Spanish-speaking population, creating a series of congregations of converts in Greater Buenos Aires and in some places in the interior of Argentina. Simultaneously, in other parts of the country, German-speaking congregations were formed, and around the war and postwar years, 1939-45, a series of immigration churches are organized — sometimes by refugees or immigrants of Estonian, Lithuanian, Hungarian origin. The Argentine Reformed Church (IRA), on the other hand, follows a different road. Under the influence of some Dutch and especially North American missionaries, it explicitly decides to extend its field of growth to the native population; it organized its resources and personnel toward that end, and in a few years (1960-68) tripled its congregations and worship centers. In other words, as Lalive d'Epinay says, that church decided "to renounce being a church determined by its ethnic origin, to become an evangelistic church directed 'to all nations.'"[31] In both cases, we see a departure from the "conservation" or "internal mission" model, a break which somehow is provoked

31. Ibid., p. 171.

from outside the life of the church by missionaries or mission societies that took the initiative to carry out an evangelizing task with the local population — sometimes at the margin of, and in tension with, the local ethnic community.[32]

The situation of churches that have followed a progressive process of "naturalization" is again different. These are churches which, impacted by sociological and historical factors — successive generations, upward social mobility with resulting incorporation into various sectors of national life — slowly become an integral part of the national religious field. Lalive d'Epinay has taken as indices of acculturation the use of language, and for nationalization the training of a local ministry.[33] It would have been of interest to include a third indicator: the number and proportion of church members who enter "from outside the ethnic religious world" the church represents — in other words, "converts." In the 1970 survey only two churches — IRA and IELA — specifically include the evangelization of the Argentine people in the definition of their mission. However, it is clear that currently the majority of the others — Anglican, Iglesia Evangélica del Rio de la Plata (IERP), IELU, the Waldensian church, the Presbyterian church — have a minority but significant number of members and ministers of national origin who do not belong to the ethnic group, and in many cases congregations are almost totally, or wholly, made up of nationals. Has this change occurred spontaneously, by a naturalization process in the church? Have there been changes in theological concepts derived from the ecumenical relation at national or international levels? Has this to do with the national training of their pastors in united seminaries, or with social changes — participating in a society which is increasingly pluralistic — or the need

32. A very interesting case is that of the Scots Presbyterian Church, which until a few years ago we would have described as eminently "ethnic," without realizing that its early history had an evangelizing and missionary intention which subsequently died out. Even without considering the missionary work initiated by Presbyterians of North American origin (cf. Daniel P. Monti, *Presencia del Protestantismo en el Río de la Plata durante el siglo XIX* [Buenos Aires: La Aurora, 1969]), the resident rural Scottish congregation of Chascomús and its pastor, Robertson, started up a work of evangelization which later was discontinued. This significant history has been recoverd and analyzed in an interesting thesis of Pastor Girvan Christie McKay, *Growth and Decrease of Presbyterian Missionary Outreach in Argentina* (Buenos Aires: ISEDET, 1974). In recent years this vocation seems to have been recovered, but not without tensions and conflicts.

33. Lalive d'Epinay, in Villalpando, ed., pp. 166-70.

imposed by economic circumstances to migrate to another region where participation in "their" ethnic church is impossible? Or were they forced by their growing integration to the national society to face social and even political problems which demanded theological and ecclesial "reflection"? It is likely that several of these factors play a role to various degrees in different situations.[34] *I prefer to leave these as open questions*

34. In a presentation at ISEDET (Buenos Aires, 1983), Walter Altmann pointed out how the economic crisis obliged many Brazilian Lutherans to emigrate toward the periphery of urban areas, or to the frontier with Paraguay, generating a religious integration or the creation of open ecclesial communities.

The discussion about acculturation, adaptation, assimilation, and cultural pluralism is very pertinent to our topic, but goes beyond our scope. One would have to speak here, in relation to our subject, of at least two aspects. One is *the model of reception and handling of immigration* adopted by different countries. In some cases there was a "harsh policy" of social, cultural, and political pressure to "assimilate" the population coming in — that they should abandon their language, their particular customs, their group intermarriage — the ideology that we could assimilate to the slogan of the "melting pot." In others a "soft policy" of bilingual education stimulated various cultural manifestations, including the acceptance of dual nationality (which does not always mean an appreciation of immigrant ethnic groups but can also be a form of discrimination). The majority of Latin American nations, seeking to build their own identity, adhered, with varying degrees of intensity and implementation, to the former model. But see also, with regard to the Argentine immigration policy, the interesting article of Dolores Juliano, "El discreto encanto de la adscripción étnica voluntaria," in R. Ringuelet, ed., pp. 83-109. Also of interest are the works of Roy A. Preiswerk, some of whose writings have been compiled in the volume edited by his successor, Gilbert Rist, *A contre-courants, l'enjeu des rélations interculturelles* (Lausanne: Editions d'en Bas, 1984), especially the article by Rist himself, "Pour une épistemologie interculturelle," and of Preiswerk, "Identité culturelle et développement." This leads to a second subject, that is, how is an "identity" generated? In several Latin American countries — as an example I take my own, Argentina — there has been a conflict between two forms of understanding the creation of a "national identity." One, which I would call "mythical," postulates a certain "essence" or "national being," tied to the soil, blood, or ideology — which could be religious — and is represented by symbols: the flag, the national anthem, some person, etc. Curiously, some immigration churches have understood their identity this way and have striven to maintain it. Another line — which, as will be evident, I consider more fruitful — is that developed by modern social sciences: The identity of a people is not a static and suprahistorical entity but depends on self-perception, an "elaboration of social belonging" generated in the conscience of a people in the interaction of objective conditions and intersubjective creation. Such an elaboration is possible in relation to an external "other" — that is, in the plurality of peoples — and with internal "others" — that is, pluralism within a people (in our case, religious pluralism). In other words, identity is created from identities; there is not only one way of *and to set forth one last topic I believe to be central to this whole discussion: the relationship of ethnicity and mission.*

III. Nation, Ethnicity, and Mission

A. *"To All Nations" (Luke 24:47)*

From the outset, the "first history of the church" poses the theme of ethnicity and mission. For Luke, in effect, there is a clear sequence: Fulfilling the promises of God, Jesus Christ "began to do and to teach" in relation to the kingdom of God. That work completed, the risen Lord, in the power of the Holy Spirit, continued extending his work and crossing frontiers — Jerusalem, Judea, Samaria — unto "the ends of the earth" (Acts 1:8). Promise (Old Testament), fulfillment (gospel), mission — these indicate the way of God's purpose. The structure of the Acts of the Apostles is determined by this route. When he interrupts his story, Luke leaves the "apostle to the Gentiles" looking toward those "ends of the earth" (Acts 28:28) that Paul himself would pursue: Spain, the *ne plus ultra* of the Western world (Rom. 15:24, 28).

Already the prophetic trajectory present in Genesis included "all the families of the earth" in the purpose of God (Gen. 12:1-3) in creating in Abraham a chosen people. That salvific relationship toward "the people" *(ta ethne)* received a classic expression in Isaiah 2:2-4. That "blessing" extending from Israel to "the peoples" was not transformed into mission — announcement and invitation — in Judaism until around the year 300 B.C. "Proselytes" were forerunners of that mission which for Luke is the very meaning of the church's existence.[35]

---

being, for example, Argentine (or Methodist, if you will). It is the interaction of these different modes that allows the creation of symbols which are sufficiently broad to include that diversity. Some recent writings have posed the topic in very interesting and fruitful ways; among them are: Cohen, *The Symbolic Construction of Community* (London and New York: Tavistock Publications, 1985); Kertzer, *Ritual Politics and Power* (New Haven and London: Yale University Press, 1989); Craig Calhoun, ed., *Social Theory and the Politics of Identity* (Oxford: Blackwell, 1994); Anthony Giddens, *Modernity and Self-Identity* (Cambridge: Polity Press, 1994).

35. Numerous prophetic passages present essentially the same message. In this regard, a good summary will be found in the article on "The Gentiles" *(ethnon)* in the Old Testament section written by Bertam in Kittel, *Theological Dictionary of the New Testament.*

It fell to the apostle Paul to give theological basis to that qualitative jump in the history of salvation which is the "mission to the nations." The matter has been studied repeatedly and, despite still-debated aspects, one thing is clear for Paul: In Jesus Christ the redemptive justice of God breaks into the entire universe, breaks down the wall that separates Jews and "Gentiles" and calls all "nations." A new era, a definitive one, had begun. We know of the conflicts Paul had to wage regarding the meaning and the specific consequences of this new situation. Particularly, there it becomes imperative to understand the condition of the "chosen people." Romans 9 to 11 is the most elaborate and precise expression offered by the apostle to the dilemma of that condition and the future of the people of Israel. Justification by grace through faith is the key, and the development of the "history of salvation" is the theological framework on the basis of which he articulates his interpretation; there is a time of grace so that all Gentiles might be incorporated into the promise, and in its fulfillment Israel is reintroduced into that history. *However, neither the former nor the latter enter by their own merit, but only by the grace of God.*[36]

In spite of the decisive role of the apostle Paul with regard to the mission among the "Gentiles" and the particular vocation to which he felt called by the risen Lord, we know that the ministry to the non-Jews or to Gentile proselytes was far wider. The church of Rome to which Paul wrote already had Gentile proselytes and possibly Gentile converts. The Samaritan community to which (and from which) the fourth gospel and the Johannine epistles were probably directed, the church at Antioch, and the communities in Egypt and Syria of which we know, witness to a wide development independent of the Pauline mission. Whatever their relationship, direct or indirect, to Paul, the Epistle to the Colossians (and possibly Ephesians) develops a complementary concept to the "history of salvation" of Acts and Romans: The unity of Jews and Gentiles is rooted in creation itself, in the cosmic dimension of the person of the Son (Col. 1:12-23). In Ephesians, it is the fulfillment of the original will to "gather up all things in [Christ]" (Eph. 1:9-14).

36. Krister Stendahl has argued, rightly in my opinion, that one should not see the debate of the relation between Jews and Gentiles as "a case" in which Paul "applies" the doctrine of justification by faith but, on the contrary, as the crucial problem around which the apostle defines that doctrine. Krister Stendahl, *Paul among Jews and Gentiles* (Philadelphia: Fortress, 1964), pp. 2, 36-37.

B. Who Are Ta Ethne and
How Should They Be Described?

Linguistic studies have made us very cautious about trying to identify the meaning of words and their usage. It is well to remember this when we deal with terms such as *Gentiles, nations, peoples*. Already the original Hebrew words and their Greek and Latin translations represent diverse interpretations. When today we speak of "nations," of "ethnic groups," and of "peoples," things are even more complicated. In general terms we can say that, in the Old Testament, the term *goyim*, which is often translated as "nations," represents (1) the diversity of different peoples, characterized by their place of origin (their "land"), their consanguinity ("families"), or their "language," recognized, especially in the prophetic tradition, as the creation of the Lord Yahweh and subject to his sovereignty — even when they do not know it and worship other gods; and (2) by counterposition to the people (*'am*) of Israel, the people of the covenant, the *goyim* are those nations that neither know nor honor the only true God. In the first sense, Israel can be counted among the other peoples; in the second, it is acutely distinguished from them. In the New Testament, though the first sense has not disappeared, the second predominates when the expressions "the nations" or "the Gentiles" are used. For that reason the early church agonizes to understand how "the Gentiles" can, like Israel, be the "people of God."

What, then, are the "nations" as diverse "peoples" — in the first sense that we have mentioned? The New Testament does not deal much with this matter; perhaps it just recognizes the existence of that diversity and, in Revelation, the presence of "peoples, nations, tribes and tongues" in the drama of judgment and redemption, which culminates in the new Jerusalem that receives, fulfilling Isaiah's prophecy (60:11), "the glory and the honor of the nations" (Rev. 21:26).

Based on the recognition of the universal sovereignty of God and the universal extension of the redemption of Jesus Christ, it seems easy to leave aside this variety of families, tribes, peoples, tongues, and nations and reduce them to a "common humanity." Classical Greek thought gave this notion a philosophic scaffolding — a universal "reason" that all human beings share and in relation to which all "singularities" are accidental and devoid of importance. The liberal tradition amalgamated the two streams and defined "human rights": equality, liberty, and fraternity for all without distinctions.

It would be thankless and highly dangerous to underestimate that "universalist" heritage. It is a human conquest we cannot renounce, today more than ever, when political, economic, scientific, and technical history has melded us into a great cosmopolitan *urbis*. It would be equally shortsighted not to note how that "diversity" never failed to claim its rights, to affirm its identities, to make its presence felt. It has done so perversely, proclaiming itself as "chosen nations," often claiming religious legitimacy and divine missions, rolling over other nations or exploding violently when ignored. Also it has done so constructively, developing its cultures, organizing for the common good, creating from within itself cooperative relationships, international organizations, and common projects without giving up its peculiarity.

Is it possible to move from the mere recognition of that diversity to a theological understanding of it? The most common path in the Protestant world has been a theology of "the orders of creation."[37] The nation appears as a reality ordained by God and, though corrupted by sin, of permanent validity. It would seem that this concept has predominated in the way "immigration churches" have interpreted their "ethnicity." In some cases, the emphasis fell rather on "ethnicity" as culture, as a "mode of being" (Germans, Danes, Scots, or Welsh), or even as "German, Danish, etc., Protestant culture." Still, even there the tie to the "mother country" occupied a fundamental place. Frequently, the residents feel themselves to be "representatives" of their nation of origin and at the service of its interests. This danger of identification of "ethnicity," "ethnic culture," and "nation" (of origin) becomes very grave in conflict situations such as those created by German national socialism. However, the equation of the biblical idea of "peoples" as synonymous with the political form of the

---

37. To be sure, there is no attempt here to try to sum up or analyze this complex theological matter. Perhaps the most careful positive discussion is found in the work of Helmut Thielicke, *Theologische Ethik* (Tubingen: J. C. B. Mohr [Paul Siebeck], 1955), esp. vol. 2; ET, *Theological Ethics* (Philadelphia: Fortress, 1969), vol. 2: "Politics," passim. Bonhoeffer reinterpreted the concept in a more dynamic way in his doctrine of "mandates," *Ethik* (Munich: Kaiser Verlag, 1949), sec. 2 (edited posthumously); ET, *Ethics* (New York: Macmillan, 1955). Emil Brunner also used the perspective of the orders of creation in his ethics: *Das Gebot und die Ordnungen* (1932); ET, *The Divine Imperative* (Philadelphia: Westminster, 1947), bk. 3, strongly criticized by Karl Barth in his *Nein* (1934), deeming it a dangerous concession to natural theology — and the pretensions of a racist state! In dangerously close proximity to the direction criticized by Barth, see Paul Althaus, *Die deutsche Stunde der Kirche* (Gottingen: Vanderhoeck und Ruprecht, 1933).

modern "nation-state" introduces, in any case, a dangerous element of confusion and the risk of "sacralizing" political, economic, or ideological interests of a particular nation in a specific moment.

If we reject the identification of ethnic diversity with "nationality" as an "order of creation," how do we recognize that diversity theologically?

C. Space, History, and Mission

The Brazilian Lutheran pastor and theologian Víctor Westhelle has presented the theological problem of the time/space relationship in his article "Re(li)gion, the Lord of History and Illusory Space."[38] When one recalls the horrors perpetrated by the "ideologies of space" — geopolitical expansionism, *Blut und Boden* — one can only sense chills at seeing the vindication of the legitimacy of "space," apparently against that of "time" and history. Nevertheless, getting beyond this first sensation and going on to a careful reading, the importance and urgency of this topic impact us. In the words of Westhelle,

> The territory of a people, the land on which we stand, the culture which we belong to, the environment with which we interact, the house which we inhabit, the familiar streets we cross, the network of people whom we are bound to, or depend upon, are increasingly and intrinsically linked to our own self-understanding.[39]

Are we condemned to choose between "space" and "history"? The author proposes a revision both of a vision of an "ideal history" separated from space, as well as from "the illusory space" which is simply the *locus* of a power struggle. In its place, he speaks — in line with some observations of Foucault — of a "tangential space," represented by the "desert" in the experience of Israel or in Jesus' "Golgotha," "when the power circle is intercepted by a tangential space that reveals the limits of space itself and the face of otherness as epiphany."[40]

It is not possible here to follow Westhelle's work in detail, which

38. Víctor Westhelle, "Re(li)gion, the Lord of History and the Illusory Space," in *Lutheran World Federation Studies: Region and Religion* (Geneva: LWF, Printshop Ecumenical Center, 1994).

39. Ibid., p. 82.

40. Ibid., p. 94.

I recommend. But I think a trinitarian vision of this subject could be an adequate theological frame within which to locate the problem, which is central to our reflection on "ethnic churches."

Creation, in effect, is the affirmation of space — of an ordered space, populated by species, a place of dialogue with God, of human communion and production of life. Neither sin, nor violence, nor human corruption totally annihilates the holiness of this space: Yahweh reconstructs and restores it for "the families" of peoples (Genesis 10). The incarnation of the Son, far from dissolving space by the presence of eternal time, confirms it. In a place, in the midst of a people, of a culture, of a political and social condition, of a language, the Son of God "establishes his tent," "born of a woman, born under the law" (Gal. 4:4).

The earthly ministry of the Son has the limits and limitations of that space, but the Spirit opens up that space toward the "other." The marvelous story of Mark 7:24-30 of the cure of the Syrophoenician woman dramatizes the crisis of closed spaces. Jesus accepts his limits (v. 27), but the Spirit reproves him with the voice of "a wholly other" — in a strange land, of another race, a woman, contaminated by a demon-possessed daughter. Jesus, who in the sequence of these passages has "won" all the debates, loses precisely this one: "You have spoken the just word."

The "universality" of the history of salvation is not the dissolution of specific spaces — ethnic and differentiated. It is not the negation of "ethnicity" as God's creation, as space for the incarnation of the gospel of Jesus Christ, but it is the negation of space closed in upon itself. What the apostle Paul rejects is "ethnicity as merit."[41] The universality of grace is not the elimination of race, sex, or condition, but their liberation for the exercise of love.[42]

An autonomous doctrine of creation transforms "ethnicity" into a closed space, immutable, that justifies itself and can only conceive the relationship to the other as dominion. This is the theological ethnicity of *apartheid*, of the "German Christians," of "manifest destiny," of "Western Christian culture," of the "mission entrusted to the white race." At the other extreme, an autonomous doctrine of redemption reduces the

41. Cf. Ernst Käsemann, "Gottesgerechtigkeit bei Paulus," in *Journal for Theology and the Church*, vol. 1 (Paper Torchbooks, Harper, 1965), pp. 108-9.

42. Nils A. Dahl, *Studies in Paul* (Minneapolis: Augsburg, 1977), p. 109.

human being to a nameless sinner, without land or people or culture or family — and, in the subjective and individualistic version which has affected us too much, without body or community.

Westhelle rightly challenges both distortions, representing at the theological level a legitimate critique of liberal modernity. He also protects that challenge from the dissolving tendencies of a certain postmodernity by indicating that "it is because of this recognition of otherness *that my own space receives a religious significance,* for in its limit the other becomes epiphanic."[43]

Have we lost, in this theological reflection, the concrete sense of our topic, the presence of the "ethnic face" alongside the other faces of Latin American Protestantism? I believe not. I would dare to conclude with three affirmations — which rather than proposals represent realities already experienced in our relations among churches of ethnic origin and of mission origin: (1) Latin American Protestantism needs ethnic churches to maintain and constantly re-create the memory of their lands, language, "mentality," theological traditions. (2) Latin American Protestantism needs that memory to be offered and received, not as a "sealed package" but as an active participation that constantly generates in all of us the evangelical identity of that particular Latin American space where we are together. (3) Latin American Protestantism — of ethnic and mission origin — needs to open itself from that identity to the space and history of Latin American society, where the Spirit of God is always present and active. Throughout all this, Latin American Protestantism cannot forget that all identity is always at the same time a creation that God loves and preserves, and the "old creature" that has to die and be resurrected "in the image of the Risen One."

43. Westhelle, p. 95, emphasis mine. There is one matter to which the author does not return and which I believe is important: Is the opening up of one's own space, by the recognition of otherness that becomes epiphanic, by itself sufficient without the relationship of that existential "epiphany" to an availabililty for the "future of God"? More simply, can there be a biblical theology without that "meta-story" that postmodernism so dislikes, but which seems to me inherent in biblical eschatology? Does not this vision of human time and divine purpose run the risk of being reduced to discontinuous moments and spaces? Possibly we have here a topic worth pursuing for a Lutheran/Reformed conversation.

5. In Search of Theological Coherence: The Trinity as Hermeneutical Criterion

IN THE PREVIOUS chapters we have tried to follow the theological development of Latin American Protestantism — the development of those simultaneous "faces," sometimes superimposed, sometimes blurred, at times opposed to each other. The question is: Why carry out this exercise? Though our work has not been strictly historical, some words of Rubem Alves correspond fully to my intention:

> The historian is someone who recovers forgotten memories and disseminates them as a sacrament to those who have lost the memory. Indeed, what finer community sacrament is there than the memories of a common past, punctuated by the existence of pain, of sacrifice and of hope? To recover in order to disseminate. The historian is not an archaeologist of memories. He is a sower of visions and of hopes.[1]

1. Rubem Alves, "Las ideas teológicas y sus caminos por los surcos institucionales del Protestantismo brasileño," in *Materiales para una historia de la teología en América Latina,* ed. Pablo Richard (San José, Costa Rica: DEI, 1981), pp. 363ff.

I. The Future of Protestantism

A. Exploration of these visions with regard to the future of Latin American Protestantism breaks down into several questions: Is the new interest in religion we note in our lands — and not alone in them — a passing phase in a historical process that inexorably leads, sooner or later, to "a world without religion"? In any case, will Protestantism continue growing, or is there a "ceiling" which sooner or later will detain its advance? Are the more dynamic forms of Protestantism — mainly Pentecostalism — fatally condemned to follow the mechanisms of routine and bureaucratization described by Max Weber that lead them to imitate the "traditional churches"? Whatever happens, what is the future of these "traditional churches"?

Attempts to respond to these questions already constitute a growing "bibliography." In it there is a bit of everything. Lalive d'Epinay already spoke in 1968 about the "ceiling." Other sociologists, such as David Stoll and David Martin — with differing evaluations — foresee a continuation of the growth. Some enthusiasts speak of 80 million Protestants in Latin America by the end of the century. In some Roman Catholic Church circles the process is regarded with alarm, at times used as a spur for its own evangelizing task, at other times denounced as an "invasion" which must be contained by all means. Personally, some requests I have received from various sources have tempted me to imagine possible scenarios, without pretending special insight, and to propose some views (which one could see especially in four recent articles).[2]

Many of the attempts to respond to this question have proceeded on the basis of a sociological scheme that presupposes as its historical scenario the transition from a traditional to a modern society; such would be the future of humankind. Once that model is accepted, the sociology of religion elaborated by Max Weber would henceforth allow us to project the religious field, with various calculations dependent upon rapid or slow growth, or other factors that might affect that transition. In summary, the end of history is progressively dawning on humanity. A homogeneous

---

2. "El futuro del Protestantismo" in *Boletín Teológico,* no. 42-43 (September 1991), pp. 155-57; "Kirchlicher Pluralismus und wechselnde Koalitionen," in *Jahrbuch Mission 1992,* pp. 19-31; "Campo Religioso Latinoamericano y Desafíos Ecuménicos," in *Tópicos '90,* no. 7 (January 1995), Santiago de Chile, Centro Diego de Medellín, pp. 11-22; and "Ecumenismo y Unidad de la Iglesia," presentation to CLAI's Third Assembly, Concepción, Chile, 1995.

world order characterized by the free market, abundance for all, a technological era, and representative democracy. It is interesting to note that the
major prophet of this "paradise," the Japanese–North American Francis
Fukuyama, has warned in a recent article that this "new world" has not
been born everywhere in the womb of democracy and — though he does
not completely like it — he admits there may be places where the "end of
history" goes hand in hand with authoritarian regimes.

The "exceptions" to Fukuyama's world surely are broader and
deeper than he is willing to admit. In a both erudite and daring work,
The Empire and the New Barbarians,[3] a historian and Third World
specialist, the Frenchman Jean-Cristophe Rufin, paints a very different
scenario: an "empire" — the developed world, rich, technological,
democratic, and educated — which turns in upon itself and raises bar-
riers in the face of the "new barbarians" of the Third World, and on the
other hand, builds ghettos and fortresses to control the "barbarians"
within its own frontiers. Meantime, a Third World persists: hetero-
geneous, characterized by "buffer states" along the north/south frontiers
that separate the world, by "surrogate states" where the northern world
has interests and "representatives," and by *terrae incognitae* — worlds
abandoned to themselves in most of the Third World. Some of the signs
of crisis recently forthcoming from Latin American economic projects,
precisely from "buffer states" and "surrogate states" — I write in early
1995 — grant some credibility to Rufin's scenario. It is more probable,
however, that reality will be a mixture in various proportions of both
visions: in any case, a confused, changing, conflictive panorama. What
place could religion in general and Protestantism in particular have in
a Latin America where buffer states, surrogate states, and unknown
lands are at the same time separated and superimposed?

B. It is commonplace to suppose that, as traditional societies enter
"modernity" — and possibly later, postmodernism (supposing that the
latter is anything but a "modernity" whose soul has been amputated)
— religion tends to weaken and disappear. The experience of recent
decades seems to question this "axiom." Already Luckmann, in his *Invisible Religion*,[4] had raised questions about the "disappearance of reli-

3. Jean-Christophe Rufin, *L'émpire et les nouveaux barbares* (Mesnil sur l'Estrée:
Editions Jean-Claude Lattes, 1991).
4. Thomas Luckmann, *The Invisible Religion: The Problem of Religion in Modern
Society* (New York: Macmillan, 1967).

gion" and pointed out that the search for a "horizon of meaning," somehow transcendent, continues in modern society, though in varying ways — with a plurality of horizons. In an interesting article, "Popular Religions and Modernity in Brazil," the Brazilian social-sciences professor Ari Pedro Oro[5] indicates at least three ways in which the religious is "necessary" in societies such as the Brazilian, with modern sectors and marginalized sectors: (1) as a provider of meanings in middle and wealthy classes — a feeling that modernity requires but by itself cannot offer; (2) as a reenchantment of the world that allows the sacralization, or resacralization, of life,[6] even in an urban setting; and (3) as an ecstatic religion that makes it possible to project oneself "outward" from the ordinary world and reach another state of consciousness that frees one from the prison of an intolerable daily existence. Even if the last two functions have their greatest attraction among marginalized groups, they are also felt as a need in the middle and upper classes. From a very different geographical and cultural standpoint, the sociologist B. W. Hargrove dedicates two chapters of his sociology of religion to the new religious movements that arise, in his interpretation, as a result of "the crisis of confidence in modern Western culture," a crisis to which those who feel "alienated" as well as those who are in a situation of "anomie" seek for, and produce, a response.[7] Among these possibilities, Protestant churches, no matter whether they maintain their growth rates, decline, or reach a "saturation" point, will undoubtedly have a place in this complex and confusing, but enormously dynamic, religious panorama. In the Latin American religious field the Protestant presence no longer is, and surely will not be, a peripheral, accidental, or "folkloric" phenomenon. Its growth has led some to hope, to desire, or to fear that Protestants will "replace" the Roman Catholic Church; that is, occupy the place and fulfill the function which that church has played, and is playing, in Latin American society and culture. Aside from the fact that I do not believe that to be historically or sociologically feasible, such an idea would seem to me a very dangerous temptation. Our secular debate with Catholicism would cease to be evangelical if it became a struggle

5. *Sociedad y Religión,* Buenos Aires, no. 10/11 (June 1993): 52-61.

6. Cf. the recent publication by Leonardo Boff, *Teologia y Ecologia* (São Paulo, ed. Paulinas, 1994).

7. B. W. Hargrove, *The Sociology of Religion* (Chicago: Harlan Davison, 1989), chaps. 14 and 15.

for power, for dominion over souls, for hegemony in the religious field. *On the contrary, it is a discussion about how, in accordance with the gospel, the church should be present in the world.* What we Protestants reject is not that there has been established, or may be reestablished, a "Roman Catholic Christendom," but that a "Christendom" be established at all.[8]

C. Protestantism's responsibility, whatever its place might be in Latin American religious life, is to offer a *faithful witness to the gospel,* which will be measured by its faithfulness in the propagation of the gospel, faithfulness in life and action, and faithfulness in the celebration — that is, in its evangelization, its praxis, and its worship. We shall deal further with this in the final chapter. Now, however, I should like to consider *faithfulness in the understanding of the gospel — that is, in theology.* It may be that theology is not the most important matter, or the prioritary question that should occupy our attention, but it certainly is indispensable. The church cannot exist without constantly asking itself, in the light of the Scriptures, about the faithfulness of its witness, about the coherence of its message, its life, and its worship.

Some decades ago, René Padilla pointed out that Latin American Protestant churches were churches "without theology." If the analysis we have outlined is at least partially adequate, the theological weakness of Latin American Protestantism is not so much the absence of theology, nor its deviations — which, as we have seen, exist — but rather its "reductionism." The evangelical heritage of the Anglo-American "awakenings," whose fervor and impact we must not undervalue or lose, has resulted in a double reduction, Christological and soteriological. Though some of the so-called immigration churches have retained in their doctrinal definitions the classic Reformation formulations, in practice they have not offered — for a variety of reasons — a correction of that reductionism.

---

8. This is precisely the tendency of sectors of the Roman Catholic Church, currently seemingly dominant in the central direction of the church and in CELAM, to take up again, in an actualized version, a new project of Christendom which, in my opinion, sets forth a serious divergence from the evangelical concept of mission and evangelization, with serious consequences at the theological, ecumenical, and pastoral levels. I tried to indicate this problem in the presentation I made to the CLAI assembly mentioned in note 2, and more extensively in an article on the occasion of the Fifth Centennial: "Evangelio y Cristiandad: Apuntes para una reflexión sobre 500 años de evangelización católica en América Latina," in *Quinientos años de Evangelización en América Latina* (Buenos Aires: IDEAS-REDLA, 1992), pp. 93-111, and *Cuadernos de Teología* 13, no. 1 (1993): 27-46.

This tendency, moreover, played into the individualistic, subjectivistic, and ahistorical character of the religious vision of modernity, ending up in some of the grave deformations our churches suffer. Thus, theology is practically swallowed up in Christology, and this in soteriology, and, even more, in a salvation which is characterized as an individual and subjective experience. It is true that, slowly, we have attempted to go beyond these narrow views. Once again, nevertheless, these efforts have moved almost exclusively in a "christological key," without succeeding in placing Christology within the total framework of revelation. *It is over against this background that I want to plead for a trinitarian perspective that will broaden, enrich, and deepen the Christological, soteriological, and pneumatological understanding which is at the very root of our Latin American Protestant tradition.* What follows, therefore, is only a kind of theological "rumination" (from *ruminare, ruminatio,* "to ruminate, to muse"), perhaps some "clues," or as our more modest Chilean friends say, some "approaches" to this subject.

II. What Does the Trinity Mean as a Hermeneutical Criterion?

In suggesting the doctrine of the Trinity as a hermeneutical criterion for the development of a theology, I must point out three risks. The first is to forget that the doctrine of the Trinity — of course, not the reality of the triune God — is *a theological formulation of the church,* which attempts to integrate the totality of the experience of revelation, not as though it should pretend to "encompass" that totality or to "exhaust" its meaning, but as a permanent "remembrance" that each time we speak of God, of his Word, of his action, we are speaking of that inscrutable and inexhaustible wealth that we call Father, Son, and Holy Spirit. The doctrine is nothing more nor less than that, an *attempt of the church;* hence, the object of our faith is not the doctrine of the Trinity but the triune God. The doctrine has the character of a diacritical principle that allows us to distinguish, to discern, to correct.

Secondly, we must not become obsessed by the "magical number" three, and transform the doctrine of the Trinity into a kind of numerical riddle — to see how many threes we can find in nature, science, or the cosmos. Illustrations of this Pythagorean manipulation of the Trinity are legion in the history of doctrine. Even more dangerous is seeing the

Trinity as a kind of "division of labor" in God, a partition of functions we can manipulate to "serve ourselves" of the "divine function" which best suits us for the occasion. Thus we have proclaimed eras of the Father, the Son, or the Spirit, or we have justified our confessional reductionism proclaiming that our theologies are of "the first article," "Christocentric," or "spiritual."

Finally, when we speak of the "mystery" of the Trinity it is good that we be clear what we mean when we say our God is a "mystery": He is so due to his freedom, for we shall never be able to plumb "the mind of God," because even as reaching to us, God remains "the wholly other," because there is always that divine transcendence before which, in the end, we can only fall on our knees.

> Holy, holy, holy!
> My heart adores you;
> My heart can only say:
> Holy art Thou, Lord!

Yet, God is not the dark, nameless mystery of some mystics, nor the "abyss" that admits no questions. The God of Scripture, the God of the gospel, is the "revealed mystery" (Eph. 3:1-13); he is the God who has named his name and entered into a covenant (Exodus 3); he is the God who has wanted to "qualify" his action, as love, justice, fidelity.

Few Latin American Protestants would deny the Trinity, but I do not think it unjust to say that this affirmation has remained a generic doctrine which does not profoundly inform the theology, and what is worse, the piety and the life of our churches. For it truly to be a hermeneutical criterion one must explore more deeply what it is that we affirm in the doctrine of the Trinity. The church did so, especially in its early centuries. In the sixteenth century Calvin and then Anglican theologians knew how to avail themselves of that tradition. Some Latin American Catholic theologians (Juan Luis Segundo, José Comblin, Leonardo Boff, Ronaldo Muñoz, among others)[9] have recently drawn attention to its importance. Latin American Protestantism must reclaim and cultivate this trinitarian tradition, without feeling intimidated be-

---

9. Juan Luis Segundo, *A Theology for Artisans of a New Humanity,* vol. 3, *Our Idea of God* (Maryknoll, N.Y.: Orbis, 1974); Ronaldo Muñoz, *The God of Christians* (Maryknoll, N.Y.: Orbis, 1990): José Comblin, *The Holy Spirit and Liberation* (Maryknoll, N.Y.: Orbis, 1989); Leonardo Boff, *Trinity and Society* (Maryknoll, N.Y.: Orbis, 1986).

cause the terminology seems at times abstruse and archaic. Precisely in this direction, I would like to underline three of these classic trinitarian affirmations which seem to me particularly fruitful in approaching some crucial questions facing Latin American theology.

A. First, we must remember that *the doctrine of the Trinity is the expression of what the Scriptures reveal to us about the history of God with his people.* In effect, it is the history within which God manifested himself as the sovereign Lord who was the beginning of all things (Gen. 1:1), whose Word originates all that is and all that will become. It is in that history that God manifests his freedom to decide and to choose — indeed, to choose the weakest and most insignificant people on earth and to covenant with them (Deut. 7:7-8; 26:5ff.) — and to "remain" faithful to humanity to the point of "pitching his tent" and "living" with it. It is in this history that the community of Pentecost receives the presence of that God as an outpouring of life itself to the assembly and all its members. The God of the Trinity is not eternal in the nontemporality of an ideal principle or of an indeterminate constant. He is the God who makes history; to believe in the triune God is to enter into that history.[10]

Juan Luis Segundo has expressed it graphically by saying that God is always the one "who is before us," the one "who is with us," and the one "who is in us." The "before" is the expression of the transcendence and freedom of God in all that he does. When we discover the presence of God in nature, in history, in the church, in the bread and wine of communion, or in the personal relationship of prayer, we are not "taking possession of God," we are not obliging God to appear — God precedes and transcends all his manifestations. There is no temple, no sacrament, no prayer, no church, no doctrine, no experience that may "contain" the Lord (1 Kgs. 8:27; Isa. 55:8; 66:1-2). As he admonishes us through the mouth of Jeremiah (7:1-14), he can destroy every temple — or experience, church, sacrament — that may become an idol. With this sovereign freedom of the God who is always "before us" belongs also the prophetic freedom of purifying judgment.[11] "With" means, however,

---

10. This is the theological perspective developed by Ronaldo Muñoz with reference to the trinitarian theme (Cf. n. 9).

11. This insight, central in the Calvinist emphasis on the sovereignty of God, is reclaimed and radically actualized in *Römerbrief*, particularly in the 1921 edition: Karl Barth, *The Epistle to the Romans*, preface to the 2nd edition, and was the nucleus of the Carnahan Lectures given in Buenos Aires by John A. Mackay in 1953, later published as the Currie Lectures: *Christian Reality and Appearance* (Richmond: John Knox Press, 1969).

that God truly becomes flesh in this world, that he does not disdain becoming vulnerable, taking on a human name in our history, coming to be our neighbor — becoming human words, gestures, law, people — a visible, audible presence. God's incarnation in history is witnessed by the concrete word in a book — the Bible — and the concrete congregation of a people — the church — where God really *is*, fully and truly *present*. The "in" expresses the very life of God in our lives, the energy that allows us to be. "In him we live and move and have our being" (Acts 17:28). And that guarantees this life forever. It is the power of the Spirit that fills the totality of our abilities and gifts and allows us to consecrate them to his service, the joy of feeling his presence and of celebrating it with emotion and a loud voice. With the dwelling place of this "in" us there corresponds experience, prayer, preaching, worship, not as mere psychological or symbolic phenomena but as the "burning bush" of his presence.

B. It was Juan Luis Segundo who, first among us, insisted on recovering a tradition of the Greek fathers, especially those called "Cappadocian": that the Trinity meant first and foremost "the communion of the persons" of the Trinity. Recently Leonardo Boff has carefully developed that theological line in his book *Trinity, Society, and Liberation*. Reduced to less technical language, it means affirming that God, in his very being, is not the absolute "I" of the philosophers, nor the unipersonal monarch who projects on the heavens the image of an absolute emperor,[12] nor the inaccessible loneliness of the "One," in splendid isolation, but *God is in himself a permanent conversation, a communion of love, an identity of purpose and unity of action: Father, Son, and Holy Spirit.* It was apparently a sixth-century writer who used a Greek term to underline this affirmation: He called it *perichoresis* — to dwell one within the other, to inhabit or penetrate one with the other. The biblical references that support this kind of expression are many, particularly in the Gospel of John (10:30, 38; 14:11; 17:21-23) and in

12. It is just to point out that E. Peterson was the first (1935) to call attention to the theological interpretations which, reducing the doctrine of the Trinity to different modes within a unitarian concept, not only did not do justice to revelation but reflected and legitimated a model of imperial domination. See E. Peterson, *Monotheismus als politisches Problem,* reproduced in *Theologische Traktate* (Munich, 1951); A. Schindler, *Monotheismus als politisches Problem, Erich Peterson und die Kritik der politischen Theologie* (Gutersloh, 1978); and Jürgen Moltmann, *The Trinity and the Kingdom: The Doctrine of God* (San Francisco: Harper and Row, 1981), pp. 128-32.

the threefold formulations we find in Paul (Rom. 8:10; 1 Cor. 2:11; 2 Cor. 1:21-22; 13:14). Therefore, with comparable energy the church said the persons are not reducible one to the other — "another is the Father, another the Son, another the Holy Spirit" — and that "the Father is totally in the Son and totally in the Holy Spirit" and so on for the Son and the Spirit. This is not an enigma to be solved. Differentiation and unity are not opposed because "God is love."

What we are shown here is the nature of ultimate reality: The life of God is communion; identity is not affirmed by closing in on oneself but by opening up to the other; unity is not singularity but rather full communication. It is in that image that we were created,[13] it is in participation in that constant divine "conversation" that we find the meaning of our existence, life abundant; it is on this model that we should structure our human relations. Neither the all-embracing authority of one over others, nor an undifferentiated mass uniformity, nor the self-sufficiency of the "self-made man," but the *perichoresis* of love is our beginning and our destiny — as persons, as church, as society.

C. Western theological tradition, perhaps more pragmatic, has tried to affirm the same truth with regard to *the action of the triune God*, coining, since Augustine, the formula "Opus trinitatis ad extra indivisum" (or "Opera trinitatis ad extra indivisa sunt").[14] That is to say, *what the triune God does in the world — in creation, in reconciliation, in redemption — is always, at the same time and in concerted fashion, the work of the Father, the Son, and the Spirit.* If perhaps it is understandable that theologically we have become used to "appropriating" to each of these persons respectively forms of God's activity, we must be warned against transforming that "appropriation" into a separation. With good reason Otto Weber cautions:

> It is only when we constantly keep the unity of God in his work in view that we can avoid an isolated "theology of the first article," or an isolated "Christocentrism," or an isolated "Spiritualization" of theology. It can be said that at this point the Doctrine of the Trinity gains

13. It is good here to recall Martin Buber, who in his brief and classic work, *Dialogisches Leben* (1947), advanced this dialogical interpretation as the basis for an anthropology from a Jewish theological perspective: *I and Thou* (New York: Scribner, 1970).

14. Augustine, *De Trinitate*, I.4.7; Migne, PL. 41/804.

its most direct relationship to "piety." It is in any event not difficult to grasp that when the Doctrine of the Trinity falls apart or retreats in the consciousness of the Community, then piety becomes one-sided and, measured by the liveliness and the wealth of the biblical witness, is impoverished.[15]

We know well in our Latin American experience the passive or conservative "piety of providence" in popular Catholicism, or the "Christomonist piety" that forgets the kingdom of God and washes its hands of the world in our evangelical community, and the "spiritualization" that loses itself in an uncontrolled pursuit of ever more spectacular and esoteric experiences in some Pentecostal groups. Trinitarian doctrine reminds us that the God who encounters us in creation and history, in the forgiveness of sins and in the search for sanctification, is the same God — Father, Son, and Holy Spirit — to whom we must always respond according to the fullness and multidimensionality of his work.

III. Toward a Trinitarian Christology

It is my conviction that these trinitarian affirmations can offer us a structure of theological thought that can save us from the reductionisms which afflict Latin American Protestantism. To fully develop this conviction would require applying this criterion to the various *loci theologici*. It would be particularly significant to do so with reference to ecclesiology, the doctrine of sanctification, and eschatology. Clearly, that goes beyond our possibilities at the moment, because it would mean considering all doctrinal subjects. Since I have insisted, however, on "christological" reductionism as a central aspect of our theological weakness, allow me to conclude this chapter by indicating some aspects in which the trinitarian criterion might correct and enrich the typical Christology of Latin American Protestant churches.

15. Otto Weber, *Foundations of Dogmatics* (Grand Rapids: Eerdmans, 1981-83), 1:393. In the German original, *Grundlagen der Dogmatik* (Neukirchen: Verlag der Buchhandlung Erziehungsvereins, 1955), 1:435.

A. Faith in Jesus Christ in the World of Religions

One of the problems Protestant theology has to face in our time is how to respond to the growing and complex religious pluralism of our peoples. Traditionally, we defined ourselves as "the truth of the gospel" confronting "the errors of Romanism" (that was our language). John Mackay had the theological acumen to detach himself from secondary apologetic arguments — purgatory, veneration of saints, Mariology — and to pose the debate in Christological terms: the contrast between the "Christ of death" brought to our shores from Spain (or from Africa, according to his analysis) with the conquest, and the "living Christ" of the gospel — the resurrected Christ, alive, near.[16] The discussion took place, however, within a mutually accepted Christological reference. That no longer applies: the new religious movements, the active presence of other great religions, the rebirth — or rather the manifestation and public vindication — of negated and underground indigenous or Afro-American religions — all present us with a new problem.

How to understand this new reality? Pentecostal growth has introduced the problem into our evangelical life, for we cannot fail to note that Pentecostal and charismatic popular piety incorporates many typical elements and manifestations of popular piety. In this regard there are already studies by Pentecostal authors, such as those of the Chilean team sponsored by SEPADE, previously noted (esp. vol. 2, chaps. 4 and 5), and the interesting article of Bernardo Campos on "The Influx of the 'Huakas' on Pentecostal Spirituality in Peru" (prepared for the Ecumenical Association of Third World Theologians [EATWOT], still unpublished), that recognize these elements and affirm their legitimacy. Is it enough that, faced with all this, we Protestants insist on repeating, as we have done for more than a century, the battle cry of the Inquisition — "All this is nothing more than superstition, paganism, witchcraft or the 'wiles of Satan'"?

We know that the church, from the second century onward, in various ways faced the question: How does Jesus Christ relate to the world of religions? We even find indications of this already in the New Testament. The missionary movement of the eighteenth through twen-

---

16. John A. Mackay, *The Other Spanish Christ: A Study of the Spiritual History of Spain and South America* (New York: Macmillan, 1932). (The first Spanish translation, by Dr. Báez Camargo, was published in 1952.)

tieth centuries presented the same diversity of approaches. Some have tried to devise typologies: Christ against the religions, Christ in the religions, Christ above the religions (as their "fulfillment"), Christ with the religions (in line with a Christology of the "Logos").[17]

We Protestants have rightly reacted against every form of "syncretism" — rightly, but not always with discernment. In the sharp words of Jesus, we have "seen the mote in our neighbor's eye" — the syncretism, "idolatry," and "magic" we denounced in Catholicism — but we have not noted "the beam in our own eye" — for example, the incorporation of elements of Anglo-Saxon culture and ideology in our own religiosity. Somehow or other we have designated ourselves as the sole possessors and judges of a pure and absolute original doctrine, and from there we have condemned the "melange" of popular catholic religiosity.

That posture, by any criterion, is unacceptable. For one thing, we have already pointed out that our own "popular religiosity" is not immune to the assimilation of elements from our culture and from the dominant religiosity in our societies. Also, only by prejudice or myopia can one deny that the biblical tradition — in Israel as in the church — bears witness to the assimilation and incorporation of terms, categories, liturgical forms, and traditions of surrounding cultures and religions. Aware of all this, some of the more lucid theologians of a new generation have begun to work on the matter, pointing out the conditional nature and the limitations of our own experiences — and hence of concepts as well — about God and faith, and indicating the need to pay attention with humility and respect to other experiences and views. The new way to approach this subject should be, in this perspective, a dialogue in which differences and agreements are discovered and in which mutual influences and contributions that come to us from culture and religious

17. One recalls particularly the debate in the International Missionary Council and the classic writings, *Re-Thinking Mission: A Layman's Inquiry after One Hundred Years*, ed. William E. Hocking (New York and London: Harper and Brothers, 1932), and the critical reply of Hendrik Kraemer in 1938, *The Christian Message in a Non-Christian World* (London: Edinburgh House Press, 1938), which summarize two contrary points of view. A good summation of the matter and an initial bibliography appear in Paul F. Knitter, *No Other Name* (Maryknoll, N.Y.: Orbis, 1985). See also Knitter et al., *The Uniqueness of Jesus* (Philadelphia: Temple University Press, 1994). On "syncretism" — true or false — I find interesting chapter 7, "In Favor of Syncretism: The Catholicity of Catholicism," in Leonardo Boff, *Church, Charism, and Power: Liberation Theology and the Institutional Church* (New York: Crossroads, 1985), pp. 89-107.

experiences, when taken up in our own faith experience, have been reinterpreted and given new meaning in the light of the revelation of the God of the covenant or if, on the contrary, they have been "baptized" without having been born again. If, in effect, we should step back from a "purist" attitude as well as from a noncritical acceptance, how do we think out this dilemma theologically and pastorally? I believe a trinitarian Christological focus can serve as a guide in this task.

What would it mean to face this matter in the framework of a trinitarian Christology? First of all, we must not separate the Jesus Christ of the New Testament from the Word "that was from the beginning" "with God and was God." I expressly say "Word" instead of "Logos," for it is not a matter of an eternal rational principle that informs all of reality but rather the creative Word that created and constantly re-creates the world, the Spirit of power and life which dynamizes the natural and human world. The *dabar* and the *ruach* of Yahweh that became flesh has neither been absent from the natural world nor from the history of peoples, as the prophet Amos so beautifully and vigorously says it: "Did I not bring Israel up from the land of Egypt, and the Philistines from Caphtor and the Arameans from Kir?" (9:7). Or Isaiah: "[Cyrus] is my shepherd . . . [the Lord's] anointed" (44:28–45:1). Or the psalmist: "You take away their breath [from all creation], they die and return to their dust. When you send forth your spirit, they are created; and you renew the face of the ground" (104:29-30). To see in history, cultures, struggles, and in the peoples' religions the presence of that Word and that Spirit is not to "give in" to paganism but rather to confess the One "without [whom] not one thing came into being" (John 1:3). For good reason an Asian Christian said: "Our God is not an invalid who came to Asia on the shoulders of a missionary."

It is no less true, however, that Christian theology cannot disengage the Word and the Spirit of God from the "flesh" of the son of Mary — of his teaching, his message, his life and his death, his resurrection and lordship. It is there where we can find the marks of the authentic Word and Spirit of the God of the covenant. By the yardstick of the presence of God in Jesus one measures all presumed presence of that God in human history — there the genuine is affirmed and the idolatry of all religion and all human culture is repudiated! Elsa Tamez is not in error when she interprets the struggle for identity of Quetzacóatl as god of life or of death in the Mayan and Aztec cultures in the light of the prophetic struggle of the Scripture for the true god. Nor, in my opinion, is Leonardo Boff off the mark when he proposes the "gratuity of the grace of God" and "the commitment to mercy and justice" as marks of a true Christian appropriation of any cultural tradition.[18]

There is also a "trinitarian clue" with regard to the question of the *how* of this transfer of meaning of religious and cultural traditions. In effect, the possibility of a genuine transformation exists only when the Spirit of God works in the history and culture of peoples to witness to the meaning of Jesus Christ in their lives. This process was broken in our America by the violent imposition of Spanish religion. Latin American syncretism is not the result of an excessive tolerance or accommodation — as sometimes we Protestants have said — but the result of the brutal effort to "erase" the history of these peoples and to substitute it by another, supposedly Christian. It is at the same time the product of indigenous resistance, the only defense that was left when the blindness of the conquest annulled the possibilities of a genuine "evangelization."[19] To be sure, the gospel never "returns empty," but those centuries without true encounter or dialogue weigh heavily. Perhaps today we Protestants are receiving (as in some places occurs in the Catholic church) a chance to recover something of that encounter. Precisely here I value the experience that is occurring in what we call "native Pentecostalism." There we see an evangelization "from below," from the life experience and the reality of the popular classes. We shall have more to say about "discernment" of that work of the Spirit. Our main point is now to submit that a trinitarian

---

18. Elsa Tamez, "Quetzacoatl y la lucha de los dioses," in *Pasos*, San José, Costa Rica, DEI, no. 35 (May/June 1991): 9-22. In a partially modified form the article has been published in English as "Reliving Our Histories: Racial and Cultural Revelations of God," in *New Visions for the Americas: Religious Engagement and Social Transformation*, ed. David Batstone (Minneapolis: Fortress, 1993), pp. 33-56.

19. This complex of subjects requires study, reflection, and a careful and open discussion, which has already begun. Of course, it is beyond the perspective of this volume to take the matter up. I would, however, point out two topics which seem to me of particular importance: (1) the relation between the transcendent character of the "experience of God" whom we confess and the conditioning of all kinds (historical, ideological, psychological, cultural) of the concrete form that this experience takes (what could be called "the materiality" of that experience) and the doctrinal, liturgical, or ethical expressions of that confession; (2) the risk of confusing, in assessing the Christian evangelization of Latin America, the problem of "power" and that of "truth." To denounce the crime and senselessness of an evangelization based on power does not mean renouncing communication of the "truth" of the gospel, even recognizing all the inherent ambiguities in any human formulation and communication of that truth.

theology will try to see and hear what the Spirit of the Lord — the Jesus Christ who is present — does in the faith of those popular sectors to make real the unity of the eternal Word of creation, the historic flesh of Jesus Christ, and the faith experience of the people.

B. The Trinity and the Social Responsibility of Christians

This trinitarian christological perspective also guides us in what may be the most pressing and debated question in the Protestant world, namely, our responsibility concerning the problems of our societies. I do not think it is exaggerated to say that the nearly exclusive Christology and soteriology in the Latin American Protestant tradition has been drawn in the frame of a priestly interpretation. In effect, Jesus Christ is almost exclusively seen as the One who came to "cleanse us" of the stain of sin by means of his atoning sacrifice, as our hymnology centered on the theme of "blood" that "washes away our sin," as "the price" paid for our benefit, attests. Who doubts that? Still, aside from the theological problems that exclusivity entails (the most serious of which is the rift much current "evangelistic" preaching introduces between the Son and the Father), it is a reductionist and unilateral reading of Scripture. No true Christology, however, can ignore or underplay the fact that there is a prophetic tradition that Jesus takes up and claims for himself. Such tradition cannot legitimately be reduced to "preaching" or "typology." It is well here to recall Bonhoeffer's sober advice not to pass too quickly from the Old Testament to the New.

This prophetic tradition, lodged in the biblical theology of the covenant, has to do with *redemption as liberation from slavery to the oppressive powers of history* — and not only from personal or collective guilt — and *for a covenant that requires the practice of justice, mercy, and fidelity* — a covenant of historical *shalom* and not only of eschatological salvation. As a result of that priestly reductionist interpretation, all the life of the incarnate Word — the teaching, the ministry, the works of "power" of Jesus — are reduced to a kind of "preface" to his death and resurrection, a conclusion in which, curiously or not, dispensationalist fundamentalists and the ultraliberal existentialist Rudolf Bultmann agree![20]

20. A quick review of the evangelistic preaching of Protestant pulpits and campaigns indicates the scarce presence of texts from the Gospels and particularly from the

The Social Gospel tried to recover the prophetic perspective with its insistence on the "social principles" of Jesus. However, the "liberal" interpretation of those principles and its inability to link them with a fuller theological vision partially frustrated that intent. In the charismatic movement the insistence on Jesus Christ as "Lord" and hence on faith as "discipleship" opened the doors to a broader christological development which I believe, however, was not able to define the deeper social contents of the discipleship demanded. Today, on the other hand, in the development of historical studies, "skepticism" about the possibility of knowing the "historical Jesus" gives way to work on social and historical contextualization which, without denying the near impossibility of speaking of an *ipsissima verba* or *ipsissima acta* of Jesus, shows us the movement generated by Jesus moving in the prophetic tradition within the conflictual conditions of the first century.[21] In Latin America, these studies confirm a hermeneutic of the Gospels centered in the message of the kingdom and the assuming by Jesus of "the tradition of the poor" in conflict with the religious and political leadership of the dominant classes of Judaism and of the imperial power.[22]

We are not here attempting to substitute a prophetic unilateralism for a priestly one but to affirm clearly the unity of both interpretations. The Suffering Servant who bears the burden of our sin and frees us

---

life and teachings of the Lord Jesus during his earthly life; when texts from the Gospels are used they are often taken from the Passion stories, or limited to isolated interpretations of some words of Jesus. I believe it would be worthwhile to have a more careful study of this aspect of Latin American Protestant theology "in action."

21. Studies on social conditions of the period when Christianity was born, commenced at the end of the last century by the Chicago school (Shailer Mathews, Shirley Jackson Case, and others), have been taken up again, with necessary corrections, by authors such as Scroggs, Meeks, Theissen, Horsley, and others. Especially the work of Horsley and Crossan clearly show the root of "the Jesus movement" in the prophetic tradition.

22. From the wide Latin American biblical work on this issue, I point out a few publications: Jon Sobrino, *Christology at the Crossroads: A Latin American Approach* (Maryknoll, N.Y.: Orbis, 1978); *Jesus in Latin America* (Maryknoll, N.Y.: Orbis, 1987); *The True Church and the Poor* (Maryknoll, N.Y.: Orbis, 1984); Raúl Vidales, *Desde la tradición de los pobres* (1978); Juan L. Segundo, *El hombre de hoy ante Jesús de Nazaret*, vol. 2, bk. 1 (1982), pp. 69-284; ET in Juan Luis Segundo, *The Humanist Christology of Paul* (Maryknoll, N.Y.: Orbis, 1986); and the unpublished thesis of René Kruger, "Dios y el Mamón: estudio semántico y hermenéutico del proyecto económico y social en Lucas" (ISEDET, 1987).

from guilt to begin a new life is also the prophet who cleanses the temple of the money changers and calls us to a covenant of justice and *shalom*. Quite rightly Elsa Tamez, working on the Pauline tradition, has summed up the message of justification by faith as "free of all condemnation" to be able to love and serve in truth and justice.[23]

If we understand Christology in a trinitarian way, we must be acutely aware of the work of the Word and the Spirit of the triune God that work in the world at the same time as invitation and judgment in the search for *shalom* and justice, before our arrival and apart from all action of believers and churches. That same Jesus Christ who summons us to participate in his work in society and in history is the one whose teaching and historical action define the content of peace and justice and who, in the power of the Holy Spirit, enables us to discern the modes and characteristics of our participation as believers and as churches in the historical present in which we are called to serve. The awareness of his transcendence does not allow us to "limit" in a social, economic, or political platform the ultimate horizon of that action. His "emptying" himself in order to assume a socially and culturally conditioned life should discourage us from seeking a sort of historical "dsepsis" that we frequently cloak with pious neutrality, but is nothing else but treason to the gospel and to our people.

C. The Trinity and the "Christ in the Spirit"

Ricardo Rojas prophesied in 1928:

> The world needs anew the coming of the Messiah; and if he came to earth twenty centuries ago as a man of flesh, the Christ of rituals and temples, today we await the social Christ, who will come in spirit, as he announced, for the lifting up of souls and the peace of nations.[24]

Could it be that this prediction is being fulfilled in Pentecostal Christianity in our time? The fact is that our Latin American Protestant tradition is strongly pneumatological. In its expression in "revivals," as in the holiness movement of the nineteenth century and in the Pente-

---

23. Elsa Tamez, *The Amnesty of Grace: Justification by Faith from a Latin American Perspective* (Nashville: Abingdon, 1993).

24. Ricardo Rojas, *The Invisible Christ* (New York: Abingdon, 1931), p. 307.

costalism of the twentieth century, reference to "the work of the Spirit" has been the foundational and basic dynamic. Yet, none of these movements developed a true "theology of the Spirit," much less a theology of the Holy Spirit in a trinitarian context. Indeed, that theology has been absent from the dominant Western theological tradition. Catholicism has not had a pneumatological theology, perhaps, as a prominent Catholic theologian recently said, "because the Church has substituted itself for the Spirit."

Classic Protestantism gave the Holy Spirit a "passive" role of legitimation of Scripture — a kind of subjective "seal" of approval that had nothing to contribute to the interpretation of its content. Pietistic and evangelical Protestantism attributed to the Spirit a role in the "subjectivation" of faith as experience. The Pentecostal movement has privileged the extraordinary manifestations of the Spirit, but without linking them to the totality of "the work of the Spirit" and even less to a trinitarian context. I would dare to suggest, in the context of the hermeneutic I am proposing, that a trinitarian Christology should consider, in Latin America, the relation Christ/Spirit at least with reference to two matters: the freedom and power of the Spirit, and the discernment of the Spirit.

In effect, in biblical language the Spirit is power, the power of God (of course, from our perspective, of the triune God) at work in the world and in history to fulfill the divine purpose. It is that word and that power that Jesus the Christ set up in our midst. It seems to me that the tendency of some contemporary historians of theology to see in the New Testament an opposition of "Christologies of the logos" and "Christologies of the Spirit" does not take seriously enough the relation between "word" and "spirit" in the biblical tradition and is overly influenced by the weight that came later from Hellenizing interpretations of "word" as "logos." This is not the place for a more profound study of the theological use of the concepts of "word" and "spirit" in the Old and New Testaments. I only suggest that, even though there are a variety of biblical shades and traditions in both cases, both notions include the two fundamental dimensions of action, power, completion, and on the other hand of purpose, will, revelation. By the Word and by the Spirit God manifests his will — that is, he manifests himself — and fulfills it dynamically in the world and in history.

If I am not mistaken, the experience of the Holy Spirit is, in a Pentecostal, the experience of "the power of the Holy Spirit." In the early beginnings of Pentecostalism in the United States the verb "empower," "to be empowered," constantly appears. Even though Spanish does not have that verb, the terminology of "receiving the Spirit" or "being full of the power of the Spirit" or "acting in the power of the Spirit" has the same connotation. It is power to witness, to heal, to speak in tongues, to be "wholly sanctified." I would dare to speak here, in terms of Romans 8, of the experience of the Spirit as an anticipation of final redemption; it is "knowledge face-to-face," the elimination of "all weakness and all pain," it is praise and full joy in a miracle and an ecstatic situation in which our finitude and sin disappear. However, this eschatological perspective remains here, as in almost all Latin American Protestant tradition, restricted to the work of the Spirit in redemption, and even more narrowly in redemption of the individual or, at most, of the church. As to anticipating the fullness of the work of the Spirit in the redemption of the totality of creation — of which Romans 8 also speaks — we hear nothing. Our Latin American Protestant theology does not seem to know of the Spirit that renews the face of the earth, of the Spirit that anoints Cyrus, of the Spirit that makes Balaam's donkey speak (Numbers 22) or that anoints Melchizedek, a pagan priest and king (Gen. 14:17ff.).[25] In other words, we know of the "power of the Spirit" but not of the "freedom of the Spirit" to work *ubi et quando visum est deo*. In this emptiness the prophetic vocation of the church in the world is drowned.

Still, this subject of the freedom and power of the Spirit requires consideration of the *"discernment" of the Spirit*. "Power" is, to be sure, a very desired "religious possession." Whoever has it — as "manna," "charisma," or legitimation of "holy order" — enjoys a place of leadership, prestige, influence. But is that possession always that of "the Holy Spirit"? This is a very concrete, and very conflictive, problem in the life of our churches.

The "discernment" of the Spirit is, in New Testament terms, a "gift" of the same Spirit, not a formula to be applied mechanically. We are not trapped in a vicious circle, for some "criteria" are tied to the character and purpose of the triune God manifested in the history of revelation. The Holy Spirit is the spirit of the creator God who gives life and protects

25. The most current view is that the "Almighty" of whom Melchizedek appears to be the priest was a Canaanite deity honored in Jerusalem before its conquest by David and its acceptance of Yahwism. In any case, what matters here is the idea of the author that it is the same God of Israel that appears in Melchizedek blessing Abraham.

and redeems it, the God of the covenant who remains faithful and calls for justice and mercy. When the power and the freedom of the Spirit are invoked and claimed for actions and conduct that conspire against life, justice, and mercy, we have reason to doubt that it be the Holy Spirit.

The New Testament established a double relationship between Jesus Christ and the Spirit. On the one hand, Jesus Christ comes and acts "in the power of the Spirit" — that is, in the purpose and power of Yahweh as manifested in creation and in the covenant. On the other hand, Jesus Christ imparts the Spirit. There can be no contradiction in these two statements, only complementarity. The Spirit that Jesus Christ imparts is none other than that in which he himself acts, now "interpreted" and defined in the very activity of the Son. To this extent — though there is no need to stick to the formula — the Western creedal expression that the Spirit "proceeds from the Father and the Son [*filioque*]" is justified. The apostle Paul also renders these criteria very concrete. It is not the "spectacular" nature of these manifestations but the fruits of the Spirit (Gal. 5:22-23) that legitimate the claim of having received the "gifts of the Spirit," as shown very well in the wide discussion of this topic in 1 Corinthians 12–14. It is true that in 1 Corinthians 12 Paul proposes the affirmation "Christ is Lord" as proof of having the Spirit, but he also requires that he who is in the Spirit of the Lord act according to the Spirit (Rom. 8:1; Gal. 5:16, 25; Col. 2:6), or in the words of 1 John 2:6, "Whoever says, 'I abide in him,' ought to walk just as he walked." Let us remember that to "walk" in the Lord or in the Spirit, in Paul or in John, meant "to walk in love." When divine power is used as a means of self-aggrandizement and domination or exploitation for economic gain, faithfulness to the gospel obliges us to doubt the legitimacy of such gifts.

These pages only pretend to indicate some possibilities in the development of a trinitarian hermeneutical perspective in theological interpretation and integration, as a correction of our "reductionism" and as a basis for our response to the exigencies of the life and mission of Latin American Protestant churches in our day.

6. In Search of Unity: Mission as the Material Principle of a Latin American Protestant Theology

WHAT IS THE CONTENT of Protestant identity? More precisely: is there a theological criterion to identify a Protestant theology? We have supposed that the classic "only's" — *sola fide, sola scriptura, solus Christus* — identified Protestantism. More technically, we speak of a "formal principle," the doctrine of justification by faith, as the basis on which a Protestant theology is built. In reality, these are rather resumés coined for testimonial or polemical purposes, with more of a symbolic than strictly theological value. To the first, tied to the adverb "only," one must always add that, in fact, neither faith nor Scripture nor Christ are ever "alone" but in a broader theological context which allows a definition of its true content. The theological dialogue of the last forty to fifty years has taught us to relativize these formulations. As to the two "principles" — formal and material — they have a long history, whose origin in the Reformers is somewhat remote and imprecise.[1] To be sure, there is in those "principles" a meaningful content which must be recovered. Paul Tillich con-

---

1. As to the history of this formulation, see the detailed historical-critical study of A. Ritschl, "Ueber die beiden Principien des Protestantismus," in *Gesammelte Aufsaetze* (Freiburg: J. C. B. Mohr, 1893), 1:234-57.

tributed to the discussion of what is the *propium* of Protestantism with his formulation of the "Protestant principle," which interprets "justification by faith" as an anti-idolatrous principle that represents "the divine and human protest against any absolute claim made for a relative reality, even if this claim is made by a Protestant church."[2] In turn, Rubem Alves takes Tillich's "Protestant principle" and sees in the origins of Latin American Protestantism the working out of an unsettling "utopian principle" with reference to Catholic absolutism, but a principle which Protestantism itself abandoned by absolutizing itself as "the Protestantism of right doctrine" and an ever more conservative attitude.[3]

As we have already pointed out, the authority of Scripture as well as the doctrine of salvation by grace alone and justification by faith have been consistently and vigorously affirmed in Latin American Protestantism. However, it seems to me that they have functioned, in a manner different from that of orthodox Protestantism: They were theological weapons employed in "the battle for souls." This combat was not just "anti-Catholic"; it was — and continues to be — the witness to a new, transforming, and vital experience into which Latin American people were invited to participate.

This affirmation does not require proof as to the "evangelical" and "Pentecostal" faces of Latin American missionary Protestantism, but I believe it is also valid for the "liberal face," though not, at least to the same extent, for the so-called immigration churches, for reasons indicated in chapter 4. It is not just that the same piety informs the life of "liberal," "evangelical," and "Pentecostal" churches, but it is also that even liberal leaders conceive Protestant presence in Latin America as essentially "missionary"; and, if they engage in educational, social, and even political tasks, these are justified as part of an "evangelizing mission." It would be very easy — and a bit boring — to document this statement with quotes from the Panama, Montevideo, and Havana Congresses, the three CELAs, and words of distinguished Latin American "liberals" such as Gonzalo Báez Camargo, Alberto Rembao, Erasmo Braga, Sergio Arce, George P. Howard, or Sante U. Barbieri.

An interesting counterproof is provided by the participation of

2. Paul Tillich, *The Protestant Era* (Chicago: University of Chicago Press, 1957), p. 163 and passim.

3. Rubem Alves, *Protestantism and Repression: A Brazilian Case Study* (Maryknoll, N.Y.: Orbis, 1984), chaps. 1-3.

the so-called historic churches (including here those of immigration) of Latin America in the ecumenical movement. In the integration of the International Missionary Council, the Life and Work Conference and the Faith and Order Conference in the World Council of Churches (an institutional integration which still has not succeeded in establishing full unification of purpose and operation), the Latin American participants have joined almost exclusively one or the other of the first two — or both. Faith and Order never took root in Latin American churches. I dare say that the reason is exactly this: Unity as mission — evangelizing and social — makes sense in the self-understanding of Latin American Protestantism; unity as a predominantly doctrinal or ecclesiastical project does not evoke interest or response. In fact, the "ecumenical" organizations bred by the Latin American churches in the continent — particularly UNELAM and CLAI, and including CONELA — hold to the same orientation. They have emphasized evangelization almost exclusively, and in various degrees the social dimension of cooperation and unity, but have rejected, evaded, or at least not taken up significantly the consideration of doctrinal and organic unity.

Therefore, if we are to discover a "material principle" — that is, a theological orientation which, as the best expression of the life and dynamic of the religious community, will give coherence and consistency to the understanding of the gospel and become a point of reference for the theological building of the community — we must speak of mission as the "material principle" of a Latin American Protestant theology. In the case of Latin American Protestantism, however, that "principle" is not visible as an explicit theological formulation but rather as an "ethos" that permeates the speech, worship, and life of the Protestant community, a self-understanding manifested in all attitudes, conflicts, and priorities.[4]

---

4. I would dare to say that, if we want to describe justification by faith alone as "the material principle" on which the Reformation is built, our observation would also hold true to some extent. In effect, I believe there is a great distance between the use orthodox Lutheranism made of the motto *articulus stantis et cadentis ecclesiae* and the intention of Luther's expression in *The Articles of Esmalcalda* from which that formulation seeks support — ("De hoc articulo [justification by faith] cedere aut aliquid contra illum largire aut permittere nemo piorum potest, etiamsi coelum et terra ac omnia corruant"). The error consists, in my opinion, in isolating this doctrinal criterion from its function in Luther's own theological Christology. "Justification by faith alone" has its place as an expression of the *was Christum treibt*, of the self-communication of Jesus Christ in the *viva vox* of the proclamation.

I. The Ambiguity of Missionary Definition

To admit that "mission-evangelization" is the principle which defines Latin American Protestantism involves us at once in the historical and theological ambiguity of that movement. What is the relationship between mission and colonialism? How is that relationship, and the reactions to it, expressed in a "theology of mission"? What would a theology of mission mean from a trinitarian perspective?

A. Mission and Colonialism

The evangelization that reached Latin America beginning in the nineteenth century is part, in effect, of the total European Protestant missionary enterprise — in our case particularly Anglo-Saxon — of the eighteenth and nineteenth centuries. Today it is commonplace to recall that that mission advanced on the crest of colonial and neocolonial expansion and carried the marks of that tie. The enormous literature available on this subject exempts me from further expanding on this theme.

In our first chapter I rejected a simplistic interpretation of the relationship between Protestantism and imperialism. In Latin America, I maintain, far from a wholesale acceptance of the expansionist ideology of the colonial countries, there is a tension evidenced, for example, in the permanent discussion about the meaning of panamericanism. But it is also necessary to ask a deeper question: To what extent has the very self-understanding that presided and mobilized the tremendous European and North American missionary enterprise of the eighteenth and nineteenth centuries, as reflected in attitudes, worship, and theology, borne the marks of the "colonialist" spirit? Just a few observations will suffice to explain what we are speaking about.

What we might call "the Methodist case" is a good example. Everyone knows of John Wesley's concern for the problem of poverty (including his attempt to elucidate its causes), his opposition to slavery, and his critique of the colonial policies of his nation, particularly in India and Africa. Curiously, toward the end of the century (1800) the British Methodist Church had silenced these themes and marginalized or suppressed the "laboristic" tendencies that had appeared within her. Bernard Semmel,[5] the

5. Bernard Semmel, *The Methodist Revolution* (New York: Basic Books, 1973).

North American scholar, has proposed an interesting thesis which he sums up in the words "liberalism, order and mission." His thesis: In the Industrial Revolution that was breeding at the time of the birth and growth of Methodism, the latter was able to incorporate into the process of social change that generated a new social class — what we call today the middle class — important groups from marginalized sectors, who thereby took on a bourgeois worldview and "ethos." Indeed, one must note that Wesley himself already realized — with astonishment and not without alarm — the beginnings of this process of social mobility and its ethical and psychological consequences. According to Semmel, the colonial expansion that accompanied industrial development allowed the Methodist leadership to channel the awakening fervor of its membership toward the missionary enterprise. In the most influential Methodist theologian of that time, Richard Watson, that relationship was made conscious and explicit. With the advent of the British Empire Christians could fulfill their mission of compassion toward pagans (in India), now "darkened and corrupted by the grossest Idolatry." These, in effect, have "a double claim upon our regards, both as benighted Pagans and as British subjects." Christianity in England is prepared for "her great assault upon the Heathen World." For that purpose God's providence is awakening missionary zeal in a nation with a powerful navy and overseas colonies. This "coincidence between our duties and our opportunities, our wishes and our means . . . is not accidental"; "it is the finger of God pointing out our way." British vessels are carried "by His winds to every clime," carrying "not only our *merchandise* but our *missionaries;* not only our *bales* but our *blessings.*"[6] What is here most interesting is not the naive providentialism but the transition to a bourgeois consciousness — enterprising, triumphalist, conquering — that the religious mission and the economic-political enterprises take on together with the same "conquering ethos." This Methodist phenomenon is not an isolated one. Fifty years later, when the United States had converted its vision of "manifest destiny" toward neocolonialism, the Presbyterian Josiah Strong expressed similar sentiments regarding the "mission" of the United States in his *Our Country* (1886) and *The New Age: Or the Coming Kingdom* (1893).

Enrique Dussel has provided some interesting philosophical observations on the "I conquer" — rather than the Cartesian "cogito" — as the constitutive nucleus of the bourgeois conscience. A study of the

6. Quoted by Semmel, pp. 162-63.

military language in missionary writings — campaigns, conquest, struggle, offensive, soldiers of the cross, armies of faith, and many others — seems to point to this religious "I conquer" as the heart of the missionary conscience. Missionary hymnody of that epoch strangely united compassion for those supposedly in abject conditions, ignorance, and destitution as the "objects" of mission, and the "conquest" of "the ends of the earth" for Jesus Christ, the King:

> From Greenland's icy mountains,
> From India's coral strand,
> Where Afric's sunny fountains
> Roll down their golden sand,
> From many an ancient river,
> From many a palmy plain,
> They call us to deliver
> Their land from errors' chain.
>
> Can we, whose souls are lighted
> With wisdom from on high,
> Can we to men benighted
> The lamp of light deny?
> Salvation, o salvation!
> The joyful sound proclaim,
> Till each remotest nation
> Has learnt Messiah's name.

In the perspective, now almost a commonplace, of the anti-colonialist liberation struggles of our century, it becomes almost impossible for us to mesh these statements with the "good conscience" of those who expressed them, but it is precisely that unity that bears witness to the extent to which the colonial "ideology" had been internalized. James S. Dennis, lecturer on missions at Princeton in 1892 and 1895-96 and chairman of Commission One at the Edinburgh World Missions Conference in 1910, wrote in 1897 a thick volume called *Christian Mission and Social Progress,* basing his thesis "empirically":

> Christianity, by virtue of its own beneficent energy as a transforming and elevating power in society, has already wrought out a new *apologia* of missions. No elaborate argument is needed to demonstrate it. The simple facts as revealed in the outcome of mission effort in every field

will sufficiently establish it. It may not be in harmony with the current naturalistic theories of social evolution, yet it is the open secret of missionary experience that the humble work of missions is a factor in the social progress of the world which it would be intellectual dishonesty to ignore and philosophic treason to deny. . . . Christianity . . . is deathless, and Christian missions at the present moment represent the only promise and potency of spiritual resurrection in the dying world of heathenism.[7]

Very few today would dare to repeat such a thesis and even less in such terms — though some prophets of "neoliberalism" and "the new religious right" seem to have found a warmed-over version of it. Two questions, however, can be asked. First, has postcolonial mission, or even anticolonial mission and evangelization, which has changed the designation of boards and of missionary personnel — boards of global ministries, fraternal workers, sharing of resources — found a theological articulation coherent with the desired change? Second, perhaps more important, have the imperialist characteristics that marked the ethos and language of the missions that trained us remained imprinted on our own native evangelization.

B. In Search of a New Mission Theology

It is not my purpose to review the development of mission theology in the last century, but I should like to offer a couple of observations before returning to the Latin American field of evangelization.[8] "Apart from a few exceptions," says Wilhelm Andersen, referring to the Protestant missionary work of the eighteenth and especially the nineteenth centuries, "pietism has been, up till this century, the soil in which missionary activity has grown."[9] In fact, it was in such soil that the "missionary societies" were born in Great Britain, Germany, France, Switzerland,

---

7. *Christian Mission and Social Progress: A Sociological Study of Foreign Missions* (New York: Fleming H. Revell, 1897).

8. Happily we have now a wide and documented guide to study this development in the work of David J. Bosch, *Transforming Mission: Paradigm Shifts in the Theology of Mission* (Maryknoll, N.Y.: Orbis, 1991).

9. Wilhelm Andersen, *Towards a Theology of Mission* (London: SCM Press, 1955), p. 15.

Scandinavia, and the United States. Some were related to churches; others were formed by individuals, though normally none were strongly tied to the doctrinal orthodoxy of their confessions. So much was this so that, from the beginning of this century, the missionary conferences, from Edinburgh 1910 on, posed the "integration" of "mission" and "church" as one of their most important objectives. It was in this search that "theologies of mission" began to be articulated, inserted within a global theological perspective. I believe there have been two dominant and fruitful efforts: an ecclesiological missiology and a missiology of the sovereignty of Jesus Christ and of the kingdom of God.

To say it in a very general way, in the former the effort is to understand mission as central to the very definition of the church. Interpreting the 1938 Madras Conference, Karl Hartenstein well describes this view:

> "Mission" means also "church" and "church" means also "mission." We spoke no more of eastern and western churches; we spoke of the Church, the community of God in the world, and of its all-important task, in which the older and the younger churches, the sending churches and the churches that are coming into being participate on absolutely equal terms. The sanctuary of God is being built among the peoples, and black hands and white, brown hands and yellow are engaged in the task.[10]

Not everyone interprets this identification of church and mission in the same way. Anglican theologians worked in Madras with the concept of the church as an "extension" of the Incarnation, "the Body God created through Jesus Christ." The delegates from continental Europe, in more Protestant terms, spoke of "the forgiveness of sins in Christ and the new life of discipleship" as "the decisive gift [of God] to the world" through the ministry of the church. All agree, however, that every definition of the church must be missiological, and every definition of mission, ecclesiological.

At the Willingen missionary conference, in 1952, a presentation by the Dutch theologian J. C. Hoekendijk caused a theological flurry due to his harsh critique of this ecclesiocentric vision of mission:

10. Karl Hartenstein, *Das Wunder der Kirche unter der Voelker der Erde,* ed. Martin Schlunk (Berlin, 1939), p. 194ff.

The ecclesiocentric conception which, since Jerusalem 1928, seems to have been the only dogma hardly disputed on the theory of mission, has tied us so firmly, has entangled us in such a dense web, that we scarcely can realize the extent to which our thought has been "ecclessified." From this asphyxiating embrace we will never escape unless we learn to ask ourselves again what it means to repeat time and again our beloved missionary text: "This Gospel of the Kingdom must be preached in all the world" and attempt to find our solution to the problem of the Church in this framework of Kingdom-Gospel-Witness (apostolate)-World.[11]

Along Hoekendijk's line, in which the church and its mission are inserted in the Christ-world relationship, a whole theological task develops, which with different tones is noticeable in almost all missiology of the last forty years. The emphasis on the sovereignty of Jesus Christ and on the kingdom of God and his active presence in human history characterizes a line evident in the ecumenical formulations of the World Council of Churches (WCC). The Lausanne Congress and the "evangelical" stream it expresses also emphasize the mediation of the church which, in the power of the Spirit, proclaims God's kingdom in the world and invites acceptance of the redeeming sovereignty of Jesus Christ.[12]

Hoekendijk's observations point to a danger which the missionary

11. J. C. Hoekendijk, in *Evangelische Missions Zeitschrift*, January 1952, p. 9. An English-language version published in *International Review of Missions*, July 1952, p. 332f., offers a slightly different translation:

> Yet the real problem seems to go deeper. To put it rather bluntly: *Church-centric missionary thinking is bound to go astray, because it revolves around an illegitimate centre.* To say that "the Church is the starting point and the goal of the Mission" is after all only making a phenomenological statement. It may well be that we are so wrapped up in our church-centrism that we hardly realize any longer how much our ideas are open to controversy. Would it not be a good thing to start all over again in trying to understand what it really means when we repeat again and again our favourite missionary text, "the Gospel of the kingdom will be proclaimed throughout the *oikumene*" — and attempt to re-think our ecclesiology within this framework of kingdom-gospel-apostolate-world?

12. J. D. Douglas, ed., *Let the Earth Hear His Voice*, International Congress on World Evangelization, Lausanne, Switzerland (Minneapolis: World Wide Publications, 1975), particularly "The Lausanne Covenant," pp. 3-9, paragraphs 1, 6, and 14, and the presentation in section III.

and evangelizing task often has not known how to avoid: a kind of "ecclesiastical monopoly" of Jesus Christ and of the Holy Spirit, and hence an "ecclesiastical triumphalism" which, far from correcting colonial or neocolonial mission reflexes, sustains and feeds them. Still, one must ask if the missionary theology of the lordship of Jesus Christ and the primacy of the kingdom of God are of themselves a sufficient correction to those "reflexes." Do they not lend themselves too much to a new Christian "imperialism," which in the end also turns out to be "ecclesiastical"? In Latin America this risk of an "imperial" theology of the kingdom of God is in part countered by "the option for the poor" as the criterion of interpretation of the reign of Jesus Christ and of the mission of the kingdom. It was in this direction that Richard Shaull labored in the 1960s, followed by Latin Americans such as Gonzalo Castillo and Rubem Alves (in his earlier works). The ecclesiological interpretation of Jon Sobrino and the missiological one of Emilio Castro are excellent examples of this hermeneutic. Sobrino's thesis is that the Christ who identifies his mission with the kingdom of God is the Christ who also identifies himself with the poor. Castro clarifies that the Christ who reigns is the "servant Christ."[13] I think, however, that both views would be strengthened were we to take seriously a rather forgotten proposal of Willingen 1952:

> [T]heologically we must dig even deeper; we must trace out the originating impulse in faith in the triune God; from that standpoint alone can we see the missionary enterprise synoptically in its relationship to the Kingdom of God and in its relationship to the world.[14]

II. Why a Trinitarian Missiology?

This is an entirely legitimate question. It would be posed, above all, by a Protestant tradition for which the trinitarian doctrine has always and almost only been a kind of "summary" of salvation history — an "economic" trinity — rather than an affirmation about the very being of God — an "immanent" trinity. A missiologist in that tradition might

13. See especially, Jon Sobrino, *The True Church and the Poor* (Maryknoll, N.Y.: Orbis, 1984), chaps. 1-5; Emilio Castro, *Freedom in Mission: An Ecumenical Enquiry* (Geneva: WCC Publications, 1985), esp. chaps. 4 and 5.

14. Andersen, p. 10.

possibly see in our insistence on this subject a speculation that could be distracting. It is interesting to note that the Willingen call mentioned above has had almost no repercussion in Protestant missiology and in developments within the Commission on World Mission and Evangelism of the WCC.

I believe that to consider this trinitarian discussion "a luxury" or a "distraction" is a very bad "economy." As long as the church and the kingdom of God remain as the ultimate horizon of mission/evangelization, this will be an act of obedience and/or an expression of faith. To be sure, these motivations are biblical and evangelical. Obedience and witness are dimensions of Christian faith that cannot be ignored or put off. However, I believe these same motivations are strengthened and deepened when the ultimate horizon is "the very life of God" and hence the mission is not only obedience and witness but also contemplation, prayer, praise, participation — as the Orthodox would say — in what God himself "is" and therefore in what God "does."

I believe this is the relation that the author of the Epistle to the Ephesians established — even more so if read in conjunction with the christological hymn of Colossians 1:10-27 — when he places the fundamental missionary event of the first-century church, namely, the inclusion of the Gentiles along with the Jews, tearing down "the dividing wall" (Eph. 2:14-19), in the perspective of the "mystery of his will" and of the recapitulation of the entire universe in Christ (1:1-14 and 3:1-13). It is this same God who brings the believer into the sphere of this mystery, which is none other than that of the love of God which dwells by faith in the believer and introduces him/her into "all the fullness of God" (3:14-19).

A. Thinking in terms of later theological elaboration, what Paul does in these passages is to unite "the economic trinity" — what God does — and the "immanent trinity" — what God is. The key to interpret the repeated and often complex and redundant trinitarian formulas of the first centuries is to see them as an effort to establish this unity firmly, to protect it against any formulation that would deny it, to articulate it as clearly as possible, at the same time affirming the great "acts of God" and the "fullness of God" in all and each statement. Too great a "theological purism"? By no means! On the contrary, it is a fundamental affirmation of faith. Is the revelation of God witnessed in the Scripture an "authentic picture" of God or an "image" for religious consumption? Is God really and wholly "committed" in the events of the history of salvation, or is this history only one of various diverse scenarios in which God acts, reserving a separate "private" space? Is there, behind or beyond this revelation — *ad usum christianorum* — a mystery of God that is perhaps accessible by other means: gnosticism, mysticism, or magic? Leonardo Boff replies very well:

> Now, God's revelation to us is the actual being of God. So if God appears to us as a Trinity, this is because God's actual being is a Trinity (Father, Son, Holy Spirit) not just for us, but in itself. If God appears to us as source mystery and unoriginated origin, so as absolute transcendence, and so as Father, this is because God is Father. If God is revealed to us as enlightening Word and Truth, and so as Son or eternal Logos, this is because God is Son. If God is communicated to us as love and power for the purposes of carrying out God's final plan, and so as Holy Spirit, this is because God is Holy Spirit. The reality of the Trinity makes the manifestation of the divine in history be trinitarian, and the truly trinitarian manifestation of God makes us understand that God is in fact a Trinity of Persons: Father, Son, Holy Spirit.[15]

B. Speaking of *perichoresis*, we underlined the unity born of the "intratrinitarian" communication: the eternal conversation, the linkage of life that God is in himself. We must now indicate the other direction of this dialogue: its extrovert character. It is not exhausted in itself; it overflows, so to say, in relation to created reality — the world, human beings, history. This relationship among the three persons as immanent reality in God and as presence and action in the totality of creation is what classical theology has called "missions" in the Trinity. "Mission" here has the etymological meaning of "sending." The New Testament is very explicit as to this: The Son is "sent" by the Father (John 3:16; 5:23, 36, 38); the Holy Spirit is sent by the Father by means of the Son (Luke 24:49; John 14:16, 26; 16:7; Gal. 4:6). This "sending" is not an accidental or limited act in a given moment. Though it has a "date" when it manifests itself once and for all *(ephapax)* — Christmas and Pentecost — these decisive revelatory moments find their source in an eternal "mission" that corresponds to the very trinitarian reality. For that reason one can speak of "from the foundation of the world . . . the Lamb that was slaughtered" (Rev. 13:8) or of the Spirit that God "sends" to sustain

15. Leonardo Boff, *Trinity and Society* (Maryknoll, N.Y.: Orbis, 1986), p. 96.

his creation and the very activity of human beings in it (Ps. 104:29-30 — the word here is *shalach*, from which we derive "one who is sent" or "apostle").

C. It is in this "missionary dialogue" that we are included. God's "visitations" from creation to redemption, and the creation of the church, always incorporate human beings as "actors" or "coactors" in the divine mission. In this regard there is a legitimate synergism that does not downplay the absolute priority of divine action because it is this very action that enables, demands, and incorporates the "partner" God has chosen into its own dynamic. In the story of creation, that "mission" is called "work," labor. Thus the weekly rhythm of divine action encompasses a weekly rhythm in human life; the continual support and the continuing creation of God is made real in human action, which it surrounds and exceeds but never empties nor alienates. In the history of salvation, this mission is called the "covenant," an alliance. Therefore justice, mercy, God's peace *(shalom)* are embodied in good law, good government, a faithful community; the "word" or the "spirit" that God sends incorporates all those who in turn are included in his "sending."

In the fullness of time the "sent One," Jesus Christ, includes "those who have believed . . . and who will believe" in the same mission. As the Latin version of Jesus' prayer graphically puts it: "Sicut tu me *missiste* in mundo et ego *missi* eos in mundo" (John 17:18). When Paul speaks of "being conformed" to the image of Christ, or of "reproducing" the marks of Christ, or more daringly, "fulfilling" in his body the continuity of that redemptive work, he is not speaking of an external "imitation" and even less of an autonomous action of the believer, but of a participation that allows one to say, by faith, "Christ lives in me." The "testimony" of the gospel that the church has been called to proclaim is always "in the power of the Spirit." In the operation of the Spirit that the Father and Son send, the same Trinity gives "witness" of the truth of the gospel. The evangelizing mission is not an external act carried out by the church but is "the visible face" of the mission of the triune God.

The "mission" of the Spirit does not have to do only with the word of redemption but with *the total work of the triune God:* therefore, with labor, with justice, with peace, indeed, with the history of the world and of humanity. Whoever, believer or not, is incorporated into this work is "sent," as Cyrus, a Persian king, or Melchizedek, priest of the god of heaven, or the servants Cornelius sent to seek Peter ("Go with them without hesitation; for I have sent them" [Acts 10:20]).

Work, government, and human society; witness and service to the gospel; and the building of history are equally participation in the totality of this "mission" of the triune God who is "the same," Father, Son, and Holy Spirit in all that God does. *However, neither did the church err in emphasizing, along with the unity of that work, the distinction of its dimensions:* "the Father is not the Son nor the Spirit, the Son is not the Father nor the Spirit, the Spirit is not the Father nor the Son." Such formulas are not just plays on words. What have been called "properties" or "appropriations" refer specifically to that necessary distinction. God is Father, Son, and Holy Spirit when creating and preserving the world, when inviting to faith in Jesus Christ and in building the church, when fertilizing and directing history. *God is so, however, in a different way and thus incorporates human beings into God's work — "commissions" them — in a different manner.* To honor the unity of that work and respond to the diversity of those distinctions is at once the task of the thought and practice of the church.

There are precise and necessary distinctions in the way in which the inseparable unity of the triune God's work, and our participation in it in the cultural, social, political, economic, ecclesial, and evangelizing task, is at once recognized and respected, and the particularity of each of these tasks is taken into account. There are distinctions regarding the proper subject of these acts (organized society, church, individuals); the modality of participation in the varying identities we have as members of society, of families, and of the community of faith; and the way to carry out that participation — the use of power, the spheres of law and gospel, one's own autonomy, loved and ordained by God — in each of these spheres. A theology and a careful theological ethic, as well as a pastoral action respectful of Christian freedom, must attentively work at this matter. It is in this framework that we must also locate reflection on that "evangelization" which is at the heart of our Latin American Protestant understanding of the gospel.

III. Mission and Evangelization

Simplifying, perhaps, we might say that Latin American Protestantism tended to confuse evangelization and mission, that is, to reduce the totality of the mission of God to the "evangelizing task" narrowly conceived as announcing the so-called plan of salvation and inviting people to conversion. Though with gratitude we may say that task has been blessed and millions of persons have had a real encounter with the Lord and entered into a new life, we must also regretfully admit that we have failed to participate in the fullness of the work of the triune God. In recognition of this lack I now ask myself where our central problems in relation to evangelization are and how an understanding of evangelization in the context of the total "mission" of God can guide us to correct our mistakes in this respect. Certainly our worship, our piety, and our "walk" — our conduct — need also this kind of correction. We focus now, however, on evangelization, precisely due to the singular importance it has had and continues to have for the Latin American Protestant community.

A. Prophets and Evangelists

When Billy Graham, criticized for the social "neutrality" of his preaching, responded, "I am not an Old Testament prophet but a New Testament evangelist," he made, I think, a legitimate distinction but in seriously distorted terms. The New Testament recognizes a particular vocation and gift of "evangelist"; evangelization as the proclamation of the gospel and invitation to faith has its own identity. However, to separate that task from the prophetic message of the Old and New Testament introduces in the work of God, and in God himself, a dichotomy that subsequently is reproduced in the church and in the life of the believer.[16] It is hard to deny that this dichotomy has had serious consequences in our Protestant churches. It has separated evangelization from service, conversion from the search for justice, worship of God from life in the world, participation in the community of faith from responsibility in society. It has confronted them, creating antagonistic "groups" within churches and among them. We have thought we could "prioritize," on our own, aspects of the work of God; even more, choose "the god" we wish to honor — let liberals deal with the Creator, evangelicals with the Savior, and Pentecostals with the Spirit! We have

16. We all know, happily, that the genuine integrity of Billy Graham's evangelical faith led him to overcome in practice the reductionism of that interpretation. It is also true, though, that it has not been enough to enrich the content of his vision of what is "the message" which the evangelist is called to witness and proclaim.

believed that a Christian community could do one without the other, or that we could isolate evangelization and service as airtight compartments that function with independent contents, purposes, and criteria. We have even created autonomous institutions which compete to take on tasks at local, denominational, and supradenominational levels with differentiated "clienteles" in conflict one with the other. In this "specialization," the so-called evangelistic "message" of the gospel has often become a formal doctrinal scheme, reduced to a particular interpretation of the doctrine of atonement, in which the Father, Son, and Holy Spirit seem to be persons that "act out" roles, rather than the living God of the Scriptures. Service to society, on the other hand, becomes an activity "from the outside," evangelically aseptic, or a form of "coercion" in the service of church growth. This may be a caricature; if it is, unfortunately, it is the caricature of a face we have seen too often.

If "mission" is participation in the fullness of the "mission of God," all evangelization should be — together with the proclamation of the reconciliation accomplished in the life, death, and resurrection of Jesus Christ — a witness to the good creation of God and a call to cultivate it, an announcement of God's justice and a call to practice and serve it. A message that, in the midst of repression and torture, speaks of the Crucified One as if it had nothing to do with the crucified poor of history, or that amid the growing destruction and marginalization of large sectors of the population presents Jesus Christ as if he had said nothing about that subject, as if the Holy Spirit had not descended on Amos and Hosea and James, as if those who suffer and die were not "image and likeness" of the Creator — that message does not deserve to be called evangelical. However, neither is an evangelization that says all that should be said without a call to repentance, faith, and discipleship, participation in the mission of the triune God. *A truly trinitarian evangelization* — just as a truly trinitarian worship and action — *is the invitation to participate in faith in the very life of the triune God and hence in the totality of what God has done, is doing, and will do to fulfill God's purpose of being "all in all."*

B. Evangelization and Church Growth

Is evangelization at the service of church growth or of the transformation of the world? An interesting debate developed in the Roman Catholic Church following Vatican Council II on this topic. It had to do with the old theme of conservation, or recuperation, of Christendom. While some maintained that the creation or maintenance of a "Christian society," whose customs, structures, laws, and values would be based on faith, was indispensable so that the great masses might gain faith and persevere in it, others welcomed a secularization which withdrew external supports to the church, letting her rely only on the vitality and strength of its message, thus encouraging the training of conscientious, committed, mature Christians who, even though a minority, are leaven in society.[17] In Europe, the book of Jean Cardinal Daniélou, *Prayer as a Political Problem*,[18] which maintained the former stance, gave rise to a debate in which some prominent Dominican theologians like Jean-Pierre Jossua and C. Geffré intervened.[19] In our circles the sharp critique that Juan Luis Segundo directs to "a Christendom pastoral action" is well known, as is his thesis of a minority of "adult" Christians whose mission is not to "convert the majorities" but to witness to the purpose of salvation and God's plan for all humankind.[20] In the 1976 encyclical *Evangelii Nuntiandi*, Pope Paul VI tried to reconcile and integrate personal conversion and the evangelization of culture. I do not intend to enter this debate, in which complex theological themes are in play, such as universalism, popular piety, the relation of faith and love. I am interested, rather, that we ask ourselves whether and how a similar problem exists in our Protestantism.

17. This subject has also raised pastoral concern. The famous phrase of Kierkegaard, "when all are Christian, no one is Christian," summarizes the problem of a formal "Christendom" that covers and disguises the lack of a personal and active faith commitment. It is interesting to note that Karl Barth in his European Reformed Church and Father Hurtado in the Chilean Catholic church, without necessarily denying its doctrinal basis, proposed a suspension of the practice of infant baptism as a necessary discipline to recover the authenticity of a church denaturalized by a purely nominal Christianity. See Karl Barth, *Die kirchliche Lehre von der Taufe* (Zollikon-Zurich: Evangelische Verlag, 1947).

18. *La priere, probleme politique* (Paris: Fayard, 1965); ET, *Prayer as a Political Problem* (New York: Sheed and Ward, 1967).

19. This debate is published by Jossua, *Christianisme de masse ou d'elite* (Paris: Beauchesne, 1968).

20. See especially his works, *A Theology for Artisans of a New Humanity*, vol. 1, *The Community Called Church*; and *Masas y Minorías en la Dialéctica de la Liberación* (Buenos Aires: La Aurora, 1973); and *Los motivos ocultos de la Pastoral Latinoamericana*; ET, *The Hidden Motives of Pastoral Action: Latin American Reflections* (Maryknoll, N.Y.: Orbis, 1978).

There is no doubt that the traditional evangelizing practice of Latin American Protestantism has focused on the conversion of the individual and, though it was carried out in evangelization campaigns and preaching services in temples, halls, or in the open air, in which collective factors played an important role, it depended largely on face-to-face relations of friendship, family, and neighborhood. The "individual nature" of the experience was one of its most marked characteristics. Each person should have "a personal encounter with the Lord," often clearly dated, which could be witnessed to privately or publicly. It was also expected that children born and raised in a Protestant family would arrive at a moment of "personal decision" — which led many members of churches that practiced infant baptism to opt for "believers' baptism" (an erroneous expression, I believe, but the one that was used). On this point, the critique of a Catholic "massive religiosity," "inherited" and "traditional," was almost always present in Protestant preaching.

Probably a survey on this subject would indicate that this is how the majority of Protestants still think today. Nevertheless, the mass evangelization practice favored today introduces elements that give things a different meaning. When the emphasis falls on "church growth" — understood numerically — personal conversion becomes a means; what is at stake is the number, not the persons converted. The dominant question then is how to get more converts. Here appear methods for growth. For example, the theory of "homogeneous units," which really means how best to "win over" an ethnic group, a sector of the population, a social class. Perhaps inadvertently and without wishing it, we are already speaking about "cultural support" of evangelization. Another example: When the possible access of Protestants to governmental functions such as parliament, municipalities, and ministries is welcomed on the ground that this will facilitate evangelization — the introduction of Bibles in schools, or prayer in parliament, or the granting of facilities — it is evident that the idea is to use society's structures to "make Christians," and that is the basic premise of the idea of Christendom.

From the theological perspective we have been presenting — and which I believe in this situation would be corroborated by a sociological analysis — we should discard the alternative: individual or societal evangelization. First, it separates the work of God the Creator and God the Redeemer. The God who approaches each person is the same God who has established the relationships that constitute the person, and also the God who sends the Spirit who is at work in these relationships

— in one's place of birth, in the social networks that mold life, in the surroundings where one acts, in the values internalized — and in the spirit of the individual. As much in these relationships as in the personal identity that sums them up in a unique and untransferable way, the Spirit struggles against the destructive power of sin and constantly re-creates the constructive power of love. In one's inner being as in one's social relationships, the gospel calls human beings to repentance and conversion. In both those dimensions of life, the Spirit summons believers to participate in God's transforming work. However, at the same time there are here two different forms of divine presence and human action, neither of which can be seen simply as an instrument of the other. In other words, true evangelization must aim at the personal nucleus that makes a human subject responsible for his/her own existence as well as at the mesh of surrounding interpersonal and structural relationships which condition and constitute the area of existence and action.

Secondly, if evangelization introduces the human being to the intratrinitarian communion which is the life of God, it is not the isolated individual nor the depersonalized multitude that reproduces that life in history, but it is the community of love, participation, purpose: a community of worship, proclamation, personal growth, in which the participants are constantly "sent" and "send each other mutually" to the multiplicity of tasks of "the missions" of the triune God. In no other way, I believe, does the apostle Paul consider internal life and the external projection of the ecclesial community as the body of Christ and dwelling place of the Spirit in chapters 12 and 13 of the First Epistle to the Corinthians.[21] If this is so, the main and paradigmatic locus of evangelization is the community of faith, in relation to which individual evangelization as well a multitudinous manifestation may gain meaning. It is the community that nurtures and sustains the members with teaching and prayer for their responsibilities in society, and it is the community which shows by its life and action the quality of society God desires to create for all. On the other hand, sociological studies on growth using

21. The Pauline vocabulary underlines this double dimension in various ways. I refer here to a brief commentary to some aspects of this vocabulary in my little book, *Integración humana y unidad cristiana* (Río Piedras, Puerto Rico: Editorial La Reforma, 1969), pp. 42-46, and to some interesting pages of L. Cerfaux, *Le chrétien dans la théologie paulinienne* (Paris: Editions du Cerf, 1962), pp. 243-45.

qualitative methods — probably far more meaningful than merely
quantitative ones — seem to bear out in practice this theological notion;
in effect, it seems that the social networks — families, neighborhoods,
work ties — are those that sustain growth, while mass meetings serve
rather as the occasion or stimulus for decisions prepared and confirmed
in the relationships of those networks. It is interesting to note that the
relation between evangelizing preaching and the building of community
(creation of groups, classes, and societies) was what gave the eighteenth-
century Wesleyan revival in Great Britain its strength and continuity
and, according to some historians, its social relevance.

C. Of "Methods and Means"

A final observation of the "methods and means" we use in evangelization
is that the evaluation criterion of methods and means cannot be other
than the very manner of intra- and extratrinitarian communication of
God's Self, communication in love and freedom. When the church
rejected all forms of "subordinationism" of the Son or the Spirit, it did
not reject the relations of Father, Son, and Spirit but rather the concept
of those relations as external authority, coercion, or blind obedience,
and it affirmed them as relations of love, freedom, unity of purpose,
what Paul called "submitting to each other in love." We find the paradigm of this communication admirably illustrated in the Lord's ministry; the parable and conversation, including discussion and debate, are
the instruments of communication of the gospel. They honor truth,
respect the integrity of communication and the freedom of participants.
Thus has God chosen to approach his creation.

However, that is not always the way we approach those to whom
we wish to communicate the gospel. I am not thinking now mainly of
the brutal missionary methods of the conquest, but I do ask myself if
some of the methods and means we Protestants use today foster the
climate of freedom, respect the ability to reflect and decide, and manifest
true confidence in the presence of the Holy Spirit. At what point does
the spontaneous expression of emotion produced by being in the presence of, and receiving, the Spirit of the Lord become a manipulation of
collective and mass phenomena? Is the message of free grace of God in
Jesus Christ we proclaim compatible with the compulsive and strident
invocation of God that seems more to be a magical incantation than a

prayer to the Father? What about the exaltation of the "evangelist with powers," which (of course!) he/she formally attributes to God — "I am only an instrument!" — but whose propaganda really claims to be linked to his/her person? Is this the attitude of a "messenger" who seeks to be transparent, to disappear behind his/her message, to proclaim the Lord and not himself/herself? What are the limits to the use of mass communication media, stagings, and shows, whose efficiency to diminish the exercise of the ability of reflection and personal decision we all know? Do not our prayers often seem more like the imprecations of the prophets of Baal rather than the simple and serene invocation of Elijah? Is it enough to "baptize" all these things, saying they are "at the Lord's service," or still worse, to justify them simply "because they produce results"?

I do not presume to be able to answer these questions, which are decidedly critical of some of our Protestant practices. Even less do I question the sincerity of those who use them, or the power of the Spirit to work, even in spite of them. In reality, little could we hope for if the Spirit did not work "in spite of ourselves" each time we attempt to announce the gospel! I do not pretend to transform evangelization into an intellectual communication, which would appear "neutral," cold, and "respectably bourgeois." Surely there is more evangelical truth in a spontaneous shout of "Hallelujah!" than in many apologetic arguments. Also, there is a legitimate use of "instrumental reason" that points to efficient methods and means which are compatible with the evangelizing purpose. My concern arises when that "instrumental reason" becomes autonomous and replaces the "evangelical reason" which is born of the divine life itself and of "God's pedagogy" in his mission.

Probably this is an adequate place to conclude these conversations. We enter here into the pastoral realm, which deserves a more careful, wider, and more expert consideration than I can offer. My concern is that this consideration maintain a constant relationship with the heart of our faith — that the evangelical fervor of our Latin American Protestantism be affirmed, purified, and expressed from within the fullness of the evangelical faith in God, One and triune: Father, Son, and Holy Spirit.

Index